RECRUIT OR DIE

RECRUIT OR DIE

◆

HOW ANY BUSINESS
CAN BEAT THE BIG GUYS
IN THE WAR FOR YOUNG TALENT

◆

Chris Resto, Ian Ybarra,
and Ramit Sethi

A Lark Production

PORTFOLIO

PORTFOLIO

Published by the Penguin Group

Penguin Group (USA) Inc., 375 Hudson Street,
New York, New York 10014, U.S.A.
Penguin Group (Canada), 90 Eglinton Avenue East, Suite 700,
Toronto, Ontario, Canada M4P 2Y3 (a division of Pearson Penguin Canada Inc.)
Penguin Books Ltd, 80 Strand, London WC2R 0RL, England
Penguin Ireland, 25 St. Stephen's Green, Dublin 2, Ireland
(a division of Penguin Books Ltd)
Penguin Books Australia Ltd, 250 Camberwell Road, Camberwell,
Victoria 3124, Australia (a division of Pearson Australia Group Pty Ltd)
Penguin Books India Pvt Ltd, 11 Community Centre,
Panchsheel Park, New Delhi - 110 017, India
Penguin Group (NZ), 67 Apollo Drive, Mairangi Bay,
Auckland 1311, New Zealand (a division of Pearson New Zealand Ltd)
Penguin Books (South Africa) (Pty) Ltd, 24 Sturdee Avenue,
Rosebank, Johannesburg 2196, South Africa

Penguin Books Ltd, Registered Offices:
80 Strand, London WC2R 0RL, England

First published in 2007 by Portfolio,
a member of Penguin Group (USA) Inc.

1 3 5 7 9 10 8 6 4 2

Peace Corps public service announcement: Peace Corps, Magnum Photos

Chris Resto will donate his portion of the royalties from *Recruit or Die* to the
Massachusetts Institute of Technology Undergraduate Practice Opportunities Program.

LIBRARY OF CONGRESS CATALOGING-IN-PUBLICATION DATA
Resto, Chris.
Recruit or die : how any business can beat the big guys in the war for young
talent / Chris Resto, Ian Ybarra and Ramit Sethi.
    p.   cm.
Includes index.
ISBN 978-1-59184-161-6
1. Employees—Recruiting—United States.   2. College graduates—
Employment—United States.   3. Employee selection.   I. Ybarra, Ian.
II. Sethi, Ramit.   III. Title.
HF5549.5.R44R47 2007
658.3'111—dc22   2007004021

Printed in the United States of America
Set in Janson Text

Designed by Victoria Hartman

To the students, staff, faculty, employers, and friends who made the MIT School of Engineering's Undergraduate Practice Opportunities Program (UPOP) possible

FOREWORD

A few years ago, I saw a student enter our career center and sign in for an interview with a recruiter from a prestigious investment bank. He looked every bit the part of a top candidate, sporting a conservative gray suit, freshly starched shirt, and silk tie. That is, until I looked down and noticed his bare toes protruding from a pair of summertime flip-flops.

As an employer or university professional, you may have observed situations like this before. Such stories always offer a chuckle, but they often make us a bit sad, too. Sad for that student who realized that investment banking wasn't a good fit, but felt compelled to follow the pack. And sad for the many students the employer passed over for interviews who would have jumped at the chance to show up fully prepared and appropriately dressed.

Surprisingly, many employers are like that young man in the career center. At first glance, these employers seem prepared, but look closer and you discover that they have little idea how to connect with the right students. They're following the lead of other employers and just going through the motions. Metaphorically, they're showing up in flip-flops.

If you want to compete in today's fast-paced, high-stakes war for young talent, you had better be ready. *Recruit or Die* is the field manual to get you there. This book will help you get inside the minds of Millennials, the new generation that possesses very different aspirations and values than our beloved Boomers or Gen Y'ers. It will also help you develop new, innovative, and timely ways to capture the attention of top talent on campus. And it will help you make the most of traditional recruiting tactics such as career fairs and information sessions.*

In this book, Chris Resto, Ian Ybarra, and Ramit Sethi give you a backstage pass to see how the masters work, with numerous stories and examples of how famed talent-seeking machines like Microsoft, McKinsey & Company, Goldman Sachs, and many other organizations manage to recruit the best. Better still, they discuss numerous ways to win, even if your budget and brand isn't as big as Google's. (And whose is?)

No one set of recruiting strategies will work for every employer. Get your team to read *Recruit or Die* to learn what others have done, and use the book as a backdrop for developing a unique strategy that fits your vision.

Who knows, if it's in concert with your culture and your recruiting message, maybe wearing flip-flops is what you need to do after all.

Sheila J. Curran
Fannie Mitchell Executive Director,
Duke University Career Center
Coauthor, *Smart Moves for Liberal Arts Grads:*
Finding a Path to Your Perfect Career
www.smartmovesbook.com

---

* A note to higher education professionals: You probably know most of this from experience, but even I learned a few new things from reading *Recruit or Die*. Besides, any resource that helps employers recruit more effectively will ultimately produce more and better opportunities for your students. And it's always about the students.

CONTENTS

Foreword   vii

Introduction   1

PART ONE • Prospects: What Makes Them Tick?   9

  1. Their Lives Are Their Careers   13

  2. Habitually Wooed and Gladly Dazzled   33

  3. Gossip Hounds and Constant Communicators   65

**PART TWO • The Recruiting Machine: Execution
Separates the Winners from the Losers**   81

  4. Identify and Attract: Beating the Brush for
Your Best Prospects   87

  5. Improving Your Recruiting Staples: Career Fairs,
Info Sessions, and Job Postings   114

6. Making the Sale: The Interview and Offer Process   136

7. The Long Honeymoon   160

8. The Feedback Loop   185

PART THREE • Your Recruiting Strategy:
A Successful Company Leads to Good Recruiting, and
Good Recruiting Leads to a Successful Company   197

9. Define Yourself and Your Goals   201

10. Build Your Team and Go   217

PART FOUR • Free Consulting   227

Appendix   243

Acknowledgments   261

Index   265

RECRUIT OR DIE

Introduction

GAME DAY

On any fall Saturday afternoon, take a stroll through campus at Florida State, Notre Dame, or any other school with a great football program, and you witness a classic collegiate scene: masses of students, with school colors from head to toe, making their way to the stadium. The crisp air fills with the fans' anticipation of the coming three hours, which they will spend cheering the home team to victory. In the night to follow, they will celebrate victory by doing what students do in college. It's game day, and there's nothing else like it.

At the Massachusetts Institute of Technology (MIT), whose athletic teams are nonscholarship Division III, there's no game-day atmosphere when archrival football teams come to town. However, when companies like Microsoft, McKinsey & Company, and Goldman Sachs come to recruit, it's game day of another sort. But for the freshly pressed suits and leather résumé folders, you'd never know the difference.

On recruiting "game day," the campus is abuzz: Even first-term students who barely knew enough to get into college are talking about how to get a job. Hundreds of them walk toward the nearby four-star hotel, where the recruiting will take place. On the way, students stop in my office to ask how they look. Good, I used to tell them. But that never had the same effect as what I say now: "You look great—good enough for McKinsey."

Incredibly, each information session hosted by one of these big-time employers may yield as many as 1,000 applications for only about 10 positions. When offers are extended by an exceptional firm like McKinsey or Microsoft or Goldman Sachs, students almost always accept them. The companies, content with their annual recruits, retire to their high-walled offices until the next year, when they emerge once again to coax the next batch of MIT's best and brightest to join them. Every year, the same process is repeated at schools across the country. In a very real way, Microsoft, McKinsey, and Goldman Sachs are the big guys of college recruiting.

My name is Chris Resto. After recruiting and managing new college graduates at Gemini Consulting (now Capgemini), a European strategy consulting firm, I returned to MIT (where I did my undergraduate studies) to launch a professional development and internship program for sophomore engineering students. It's called the MIT Undergraduate Practice Opportunities Program (UPOP), and I serve as its director.

Here my staff and I have worked closely with more than 1,000 undergraduates since 2001—teaching them skills in interviewing, etiquette, and networking to prepare them for their first foray into the workplace.

We also work with employers to place our students in summer internships. We have engaged representatives from more than 1,500 corporations and nonprofits, developing relationships with people from all levels of college recruiting: frontline recruiters, HR professionals, hiring managers, direct bosses, intern buddies and mentors, and senior executives. We even visit many of these job sites to see how the students and companies are interacting.

This position, combined with my experience at Gemini Consulting, has given me unique insight into both sides of the war for young talent. And because I am in constant, year-round contact with students and employers, I serve as a trusted advisor and confidant to both parties, helping students win employment and employers woo young recruits—for both internships and full-time jobs, since they involve very much the same elements.

As I help employers navigate the waters of college recruiting, I find much of my time is devoted to explaining how things have changed: how today's college students don't simply feel lucky to have a job, as students did twenty years ago, but that their internships during college and their entry-level positions after graduation must be great and glamorous next steps in their already lengthy and accomplished "careers"; how they gossip about employers and the recruiting process as fast and furiously as cell phones and Facebook will let them; how the bar for world-class recruiting has been pushed so high that the traditional find-to-sign process is now only one of the *four* components of the recruiting machines run by the best recruiting organizations.

And, most disturbingly of all, how the war for young talent has fast become winner take all.

While hundreds of students might attend events by employers like Microsoft, McKinsey, and Goldman Sachs, other firms often draw a mere 20. While the top firms may get as many as 1,000 applicants, other companies may get as few as a dozen. And when interviews roll around, students often simply fail to show up for companies second in reputation or size.

In this book we'll discuss all that and more.

COLLEGE RECRUITING MATTERS

Why does college recruiting even matter? Why should any organization take pains to identify, attract, and hire today's best and brightest—especially if they might leave after only two or three years? Bill Gates, the cofounder of Microsoft, has said that "young people are more willing to learn, come up with new ideas." A number of Microsoft recruiters have told me that Bill Gates's focus on recruiting is pivotal to the company. In fact, Gates believes recruiting top talent is so important that he personally scouts a few graduating seniors every year. Like Gates, most company recruiters are attracted to young prospects because of their contagious energy, fresh perspective, and abundant ambition.

David Cirnigliaro, a former senior manager in Capgemini's strategy consulting division, says it's even more concrete than that. Young talent helps the bottom line. "Very often, having bright, new college graduates . . . is what makes them profitable. Frankly, we can pay them less than half the salary of their MBA counterparts, and they often can do the same work. But not just every undergraduate has that kind of ability. That's why we put so much effort into getting the top candidates we want."

I recently spoke with the head recruiter of a large communications company about how she was doing at MIT. Extremely pleased, she said, "The 20 students who applied for this last round of interviews are really great." While those 20 students were good, I knew firsthand that the best MIT students had not even bothered to apply. Like many employers I advise, she simply had no idea what she was missing.

As more employers catch on, college recruiting is fast becoming the hottest area of the labor market today. According to the National Association of Colleges and Employers, entry-level hiring on college campuses increased nearly 13.8 percent in 2005–06 and another 17.4 percent in 2006–07. Across the country, campuses are seeing a 20 to 30 percent increase in the number of employers attending their career fairs and soliciting résumés. Last year when Rick Deodato, a recruiter for General Atomics, called career fair organizers at Virginia Tech one day after registration opened, he was turned away. There simply wasn't any room.

The problem will drastically worsen. By 2014, the American economy will have six million degreed candidates *fewer* than the jobs we need to fill, according to the Employment Policy Foundation's ninth annual workplace report.

The importance of human capital—of finding the best—sounds obvious, but we have spoken to dozens of HR professionals who are constantly fighting within their organizations for more resources to do the job right. Now, more than ever, recruiting strategies are critically important. In *Recruit or Die*, we'll show you how the best seize the best—and how you can, too.

WHY MICROSOFT, MCKINSEY, AND GOLDMAN SACHS?

Many organizations do a fine job recruiting on college campuses. What makes Microsoft, McKinsey, and Goldman Sachs so special?

Few organizations have demonstrated as massive a commitment as these three to recruiting the best and brightest. Few other firms have engaged in such a systematic, nationwide recruiting strategy. And a remarkably small number of firms have achieved such stellar results through several economic booms and busts.

Microsoft, McKinsey, and Goldman are dominant in attracting, recruiting, and hiring. In other words, they get the candidates they want.

How? You may think: *They have a great brand*, or *They have so much money*. You may even believe that these firms have become such superpowers that they don't have to work very hard for success.

It's true that having a well-known brand, a healthy supply of resources, and a leading position in its industry doesn't hurt the recruiting efforts of an organization. But the four keys to the recruiting prowess of Microsoft, McKinsey, and Goldman Sachs are entirely different. Understanding and using these keys can help any company unlock the secrets to successful superstar recruiting.

1. **They won't settle for anyone other than exactly the recruits they want.**

   They live and breathe the mind-set that talent is everything, and it is that fierce resolve that drives them to create the best recruiting teams, strategies, and standards—period. If Microsoft, McKinsey, or Goldman Sachs has an interview round in which no candidate really wows them, no one is hired. Even if recruits get through Microsoft's rigorous screening process and work as summer interns in Redmond, Washington, there's still a good chance they won't be asked to return for another internship or full-time work. Microsoft keeps only the best.

2. **They work harder and smarter than their competitors to know their target audience: the recruits.**

   It's easy to point to dominant companies and shrug your shoulders in self-pity. But what these whiners don't acknowledge is that Goldman Sachs calls every few weeks to ask about the latest campus buzz. And Goldman doesn't care if the buzz is related to jobs or not. They're constantly monitoring the student pulse on campus, trying to gain a competitive advantage through better intelligence about today's top college graduates. When are midterm exams? What happened at the game last week? What are students on Facebook talking about right now?

   This approach takes effort, although it's not expensive; there's room in your budget for a telephone call, right? That's harder *but* smarter.

3. **They sell themselves better than their competitors do.**

   In professional services, people are the only asset. If a firm's staff can't sell the firm and themselves to clients, the firm is dead. As a result, people from McKinsey and Goldman

Sachs have more practice selling themselves than people from firms like General Motors or Boeing, where employees are trained to sell products, not people, leaving them at a disadvantage when it comes time to recruit students on campus. Still, this disadvantage can be overcome when a company becomes conscious of the need to sell itself. Just remember: Your company is always marketing, whether through the HR channel, your Web site, or through a chance interaction between a college student and one of your employees. And your potential recruits are listening.

4. They present a united front.

Because recruiting requires the involvement and coordination of so many players from so many different parts of an organization, inevitably, it's infighting that holds most employers back. But when Microsoft, McKinsey, or Goldman Sachs hit a snag (yes, they do make mistakes from time to time), their people pull together to correct the situation and move on. I've seen it. I know it happens. And to outsiders? All they see is a singularly united perspective.

Recruit or Die is not focused on only these three companies. We use Microsoft, McKinsey, and Goldman Sachs as marquee examples, but we draw from hundreds of other companies' tactics to lay out the best ways to win the recruiting battle. We'll show you how to use these best practices to understand the motivational psychology of your prospects, to beat your competition in all stages of the college recruiting process, and to create your own finely tuned recruiting machine, even on a shoestring budget.

To ensure that *Recruit or Die* provides you with the authentic student perspective that you absolutely must understand to transform your recruiting, I teamed up with Ian Ybarra and Ramit Sethi, two top recent graduates who understand this topic better than anyone.

Ian, a professional writer and MIT graduate, helped me launch UPOP when he was in college and has since helped hundreds of students discover the work they love. Ramit, a Stanford graduate, wondered why so many of his peers were being recruited to the same few companies. After interviewing with dozens of companies himself, he turned the tables and started interviewing *them*. Together, we've spoken informally with thousands of students and formally surveyed a thousand more. We'll show you how to work harder and smarter than your competitors to get inside the heads of today's top recruits. We'll show you how to start selling your organization by selling your people like never before.

Once you put into practice the lessons in *Recruit or Die*, you won't have to settle for recruits passed over by stalwarts like Microsoft, McKinsey, or Goldman Sachs. Your company is small? Unknown? Low on a recruiting budget? It doesn't matter. Even you can beat the big guys in the war for young talent.

—Chris Resto

◆ PART ONE ◆

PROSPECTS

What Makes Them Tick?

Every year Microsoft recruiters visit more than 50 colleges across the country, most of them multiple times. This gives Microsoft a presence on campus and the chance to get to know their prospects inside and out. Recruiters discover what motivates them, what's attractive to them, what their habits, tastes, dreams, and fears are. Intentionally, Microsoft's recruiters are mostly young, smart, and appealing themselves, so they move easily among their own prospects, gathering valuable intelligence and acting as a living advertisement for the culture and climate at Microsoft. If you're not working from a real, practical, grassroots awareness of who these prospects are and where they're coming from, you may as well be speaking another language. And walking away with no hires.

A national lab recently tried to recruit at MIT and failed miserably because its representatives didn't spend one minute thinking about who their target audience was. To announce their presence the recruiters bought a small ad in the campus newspaper, with no message beyond "Come work for us." Then they sent an extremely boring speaker to deliver the information session. He was a nice, experienced guy—thirty years with the lab—who was working on an exciting defense technology. But you wouldn't know from hearing him speak that he was excited about it. He failed to discuss what interns or new hires would encounter on the job, what was in it for them, what their living arrangements would be for the summer, and how many other young people worked at the lab—all "must-know" details for the students. And because his organization didn't care to know whom they were recruiting, more students walked out of the room during his talk than applied for the two jobs he was trying to fill.

Once you know what Microsoft and McKinsey already know about today's recruits—that they are obsessed with achievement and are deeply invested in their careers, that they crave glamour and love gossip—you might be inclined to think these kids are just too fussy and difficult to work with. But make no mistake, this generation possesses certain energies, creativities, and talents you won't find anywhere else. And if you want to recruit them successfully, you have to get into their heads.

1

Their Lives Are Their Careers

Top college graduates aren't just looking for their first jobs. They're looking to accelerate their careers. What? You may be asking yourself how that can be if a college graduate's career hasn't even begun! But that's not how today's students see things. Since they graduated from high school—and even before that—they have been making strategic decisions like which classes to take and which sports teams and clubs to join, all in an effort to craft academic journeys that will propel them to success. They see this as the first phase of their careers and of their adult lives.

Choosing a college was the last major decision these recruits made, and how the students went about doing that provides great insight into how they will evaluate potential employers. Culture, location, facilities, curriculum, quality of teaching, and, of course, the price tag are all factors involved in choosing a college. But one question trumps all other criteria in the minds of students and their parents: Which college is going to open the most doors upon graduation?

Whether you're trying to get top high school students to attend your college or top college students to work for your organization, it's not enough to offer your recruits a great place to be. You must offer them an even better place to be *from*. This is why high school students fight tooth and nail to get into Harvard, to share a pedigree with the successful people who have gone before them: authors, movie stars, Nobel laureates, business tycoons, presidents.

Companies like Microsoft and McKinsey are the Harvards of the corporate world. Top recruits see them as great places to *be*, because Microsoft and McKinsey promise to help recruits develop top-notch professional skills, get exposure to new industries, products, and job functions, and learn from a plethora of smart and motivated people. But recruits also see Microsoft and McKinsey as even better places to be *from*, because one of those names on your résumé means the world thinks you're pretty special.

The good news is that Microsoft and McKinsey are not the only good places to be and to be from. (Your organization is pretty great, too, isn't it?) But, sadly, today's college recruiting battles are lopsided in favor of employers like Microsoft, McKinsey, and Goldman Sachs because they're the only companies saying what top recruits want to hear. This chapter will help you change that. You'll discover how your most desired recruits think about this next and important stage of their careers. You'll learn to avoid the biggest mistake most employers make. And you'll find many ways to show you will care for recruits' careers so that they may confidently make your organization their next stop—which gives you the opportunity to keep them for even longer into their professional lives!

YOUNG AND CONFUSED, YET ABSOLUTELY CERTAIN

While their youth and limited exposure to professional life makes it natural for students to be confused about what to do with their working lives, your target recruits are absolutely certain about one thing: They want to be tomorrow's leaders and they want to change the world in profound ways. They think it's their destiny.

> Most students don't really know what they want to do with their lives. So many of them (okay, myself included) drop résumés for almost every position on PennLink [the University of Pennsylvania recruiting Web site]. That sounds pretty pathetic, but I know I wasn't the only one.
>
> —John, business/economics major, University of Pennsylvania

Parents and teachers were first to praise them with a "You are the future" message. In college, that tune is trumpeted even louder. At the last MIT freshman convocation, President Susan Hockfield told the incoming class of 2009, "Your turn is next. The world looks to you to lead in designing solutions to our pressing challenges—sustainable energy, contagious diseases, and urban sprawl. Our mission is to teach you to make the world that will be and to be leaders of that world." No doubt the commencement address on every campus drips with even more "You will rule the world" rhetoric.

Now, there are two mind-sets that you as a potential employer can adopt to deal with these future kings and queens. You can take the "When I was their age" approach, dismiss their expectations as delusions of entitlement, and go about recruiting them as if they should feel lucky to work for you and have a chance to pay their dues for a while. Or, you can embrace this new paradigm and appeal to their aspirations: "Hey, if you want to be the next Lou Gerstner or Meg Whitman, that's great. Come to McKinsey and we can help make that happen," said one McKinsey recruiter.

That's exactly what your target recruit wants to hear: "You want to be a leader, a real mover and shaker? We're the place to start!" Companies need to convey confidence, even arrogance, about how the people they recruit develop into the best, and then deliver on that promise by challenging interns and employees on the job. Employers who don't use this tack will have trouble retaining motivated recruits. When Daniel, a graduate student at the University of California at San Diego, interned for a major carmaker, he spent the first three weeks just reading "background" materials before his manager took the time to explain what exactly his project would entail. The delay sent Daniel the message that his project wasn't very important. The next fall biotechnology firms Medtronic and Guidant were able to steal Daniel's interest from the automobile industry by clearly describing the work he would do if he joined them and providing examples of why the projects mattered to the companies' goals.

This desire top students have for work that is meaningful and important is one reason why starting a career in management consulting is so appealing: Where else can you rub elbows with Fortune 100 CEOs at age twenty-two?

THE BIGGEST MISTAKE EMPLOYERS MAKE

Recruiting Maria should have been a piece of cake for any technology company. She first discovered her passion for computers during middle school, and she often practiced her programming skills in her spare time throughout high school. During college she held two summer computer science internships in which she thrived. Maria was one of the top computer science students at MIT and was surely going to join a technology company after college, right? Wrong.

Like most other top college graduates, Maria was so bright she could do anything and so young she wasn't sure what to do first. While she loved the field, Maria did not want to feel like she was committing her life to computer technology. She broached this issue with recruiters from several technology companies who were dying to have her, but when she said she wasn't sure she wanted to do programming for the rest of her life, the recruiters just changed the subject.

"All I wanted them to do was reassure me," Maria said. "Just tell me, 'You aren't committing your life to this. Of course, we think you'll love the job and the company, but if you don't, there are so many different paths you can take later. We have people who've done it all.'" That's just the message she got from Bain & Company, a consulting company and one of McKinsey's main competitors. Of her signing with Bain, Maria said, "At least with Bain, I felt confident that I would be able to pursue any profession after working there."

The biggest and most common mistake employers make is leaving their target recruits feeling as if accepting an internship or a full-time job is like signing their lives away to the organizations. One recruiter at a large consumer products company pitched his company's retirement benefits to the candidate, noting that if he worked there, the candidate would have a "million dollars—cash" when he retired. *Retired.* That's the R-word to college students.

When trying to convince a top recruit to join your organization, you won't know what his entire career path will be, but you might expect one with some of the following characteristics:

- Entry-level job with increasing skills over time
- Consistent but small, incremental increases in responsibility
- Gradual, consistent income increases
- A few transitions between functions (marketing, sales, finance, etc.)
- If you have multiple offices, perhaps a couple of changes in location

Your target recruit, on the other hand, without appropriate guidance and reassurance from you, will assume you're trying to sell him on a path that looks like this:

- Time with company trumps performance and potential
- Paying dues for years before getting promotion, increased responsibility, opportunity to make impact

- No salary increase without official promotion
- Secure but not so exciting job until retirement
- A career parents may like but peers don't envy

And that's a scary picture because the one he envisions looks something more like this:

- Two or three years of entry-level work leading to a big promotion
- Responsibility increasing as quickly and fluidly as capability is shown
- Graduate school for two years to accelerate the career path
- Lots of mobility: different functions, different companies, different locations
- Several leaps to higher-level positions with big bumps in salary
- Perhaps a one-year, midcareer hiatus to travel, write a book, or volunteer with a nonprofit

Employers often get angry and defensive when they see this last point and wish the students were thinking more about what's best for the company. Time to face the facts! Students do not think about what's best for your organization during the recruiting process. They may start to think about the company once they actually begin to work, but while they're deciding where they will work, they think about only one thing: keeping *their* options open.

As noted in a *Fast Company* article on culture clashes, young recruits are not only comfortable with ambiguous career paths, they *seek* them. Dan Rasmus, a futurist at Microsoft, wrote, "They have no expectation that the first place they work will be related to their career, so they're willing to move around until they find a place that suits them."

Recruits have commitment issues. Before they enter into any

working relationship, they need to know that if they ever want to break it off, they will be able to secure a position in a different industry or job function. They want to be sure that working for you is a step forward and not a step back, no matter in what direction they choose to take their careers. Even if a recruit has a deep passion for your organization's business and industry, as Maria did for computer technology, she still won't join your company if she senses that it might lead to her getting stuck or that it might limit her future choices.

Retaining top talent is difficult, sure, but not impossible. Like the cell phone subscriber who refuses to sign a contract but sticks with a single provider for years, or the tenant who won't sign a lease but occupies the same apartment month-to-month for a lifetime, a top college graduate you recruit today may very well spend five, ten, or more years in your organization. There are tips later in this chapter for getting recruits to stay, but that's not your worry just yet. You must first get them to start. To do that, you have to know that your target recruits smell restrictive pigeonhole positions from a mile away. So it's your job to proactively allay their fears of getting stuck and reassure them that working for you is, in fact, one of the many steps they can take toward a sky's-the-limit future. To do this, you must continuously answer the following two questions that your recruits are thinking even if they don't ask!

1. **If I join your organization after college, will I have to do the same thing for the rest of my life?**

    Here's your line: "It's your life." Let recruits know that taking this job does not mean they have to stay in this profession, this company, or even this industry later in their careers. If they want to, of course, you'll help, but it's up to them. You may think this is silly, but this small admission shows recruits that you care about your employees' personal careers. And this will get you better recruits.

2. What can I do after my first job with your organization?

Give them role models. Openly discuss the careers of predecessors—even ones who eventually left your organization. If design engineers in your firm have moved on to jobs in marketing or sales within your company or others, talk it up. Describe options in such diversity and number that your concluding statement becomes, "See, you can basically do *anything* after this job."

Teach For America, a nonprofit that sends recent college grads to teach in inner-city school districts, and one of the most innovative college-recruiting organizations, makes a point of highlighting its graduates' successes. After a two-year teaching stint, alumni go on to graduate school, academia, technology, and just about every other industry you can imagine. Teach For America's legendary network has helped make it irresistible as an employer. Last year, Teach For America had over 19,000 applicants (mostly from elite schools) and accepted fewer than 13 percent. The organization has made being a nonprofit sexy, and working for it gets only more attractive to young recruits as its network grows.

Providing the right answers to these two questions is usually all that's required to put a recruit at ease. But not always.

Two MIT students interned recently with a top engineering company, working in the same division on similar projects but in two different groups. Each ended the summer with polar-opposite opinions about the company. One student worked with a group of engineers who had been with the company for 30 years, and each day those engineers reminded the student how long they had been there. Just because the engineers in his group had indeed been doing the same job their whole lives didn't mean the student wanted to do the same. Although these loyal engineers probably liked what they were doing, nineteen- or twenty-year-old kids rarely think of a thirty-year stint doing the same thing every day as an exciting, successful career.

The student in the second group had a completely different experience. He felt that his position provided an excellent way into a leadership post in a technical group at this company or any other company. Why? Everyone in his group was participating in a leadership development program. Projects rotated often, and he worked with a few graduates of the program who had gone on to hold senior leadership positions in the company.

The difference between the two intern experiences was not only in the type of work, but in the entire culture of how employees approached their work. In the first example, the intern saw a stodgy group of people working the same way they had worked in 1975. But the second group was moving, learning, and sharing. It was *fluid*, and the intern could immediately see how much more valuable—and fun—this environment was. The second group knew this, as it had taken an active role in crafting its message to recruits: "We'll give you the opportunity to find your passion. Want proof? Look at our other employees."

HELPING THEM FIND THEIR WAY

Once your recruits know that working for you can help them do anything, find ways to help them figure out what that "anything" might be. Most won't have any idea what they really want to do. How could they? Experiencing something is the only way you can truly know if you like it. They may have done internships or co-ops, but most recent graduates have never had full-time jobs. They also likely pursued multiple interests throughout college; for this generation, committing to one interest means always wondering what they are missing. The reality, though, is that we all have to make a commitment to a profession at some point in our careers, even if only for a few years. From the perspective of today's top college graduates, that means looking for positions that expose them to as many different career paths as possible.

Employers like Microsoft and McKinsey constantly expose new hires to numerous projects and challenges. They know it makes business sense to do so because their employees are happier, more engaged in their work, and more aware and involved in the "big picture." But many companies neglect to show recruits new projects or disciplines. And this mind-set prevents them from attracting top talent.

One representative of a metallurgy consortium phoned MIT looking for top graduates to work for the consortium's member companies: "We're looking for candidates who are sincerely interested in iron ore." Are you kidding? Do you know one twenty-one-year-old person who is "sincerely interested in iron ore"? At the suggestion that the consortium might get better results by de-emphasizing the iron ore industry and emphasizing the myriad job functions and industries new hires would be exposed to, the consortium rep just about hung up the phone.

Happily, new recruits are not completely unreasonable—they don't expect to do sales one day and assembly-line manufacturing the next. They just want a glimpse of as many different job functions, industries, and people as possible. They want to see the big picture and not just the walls of their cubicles. They want to understand how their work relates to the work of others in an organization. And they want to know that you respect their desire to learn more about what's out there. Here are five ways your organization can expose new recruits to all they want to see:

1. Offer formal rotation programs.

This is the easiest way to sell exposure to new recruits because variety is built into the job itself. Formal rotation programs are why every top graduate considers the consulting industry. Recruits often say, "I can go to McKinsey and be exposed to different industries. Then I'll have a better idea of what I want to do."

They are partially right. In consulting, projects can come and go every three to six months. And most often, a new project means working with a new company or even a new industry. That sounds very attractive to a generation of recruits that doesn't know what it wants to do or shies away from commitment. But consulting is not the only industry that successfully employs rotation programs. General Electric has programs for new hires throughout all of its divisions, with new recruits rotating every few months to a new part of the business. Intuit offers rotation programs in finance, customer service, product development, and marketing; new recruits rotate to a new part of the business every six to twelve months. An added bonus for young recruits is that these rotation programs are well known as feeders for the companies' leadership positions.

2. Feature special project assignments.

For most organizations, rotating staff is difficult, but winning companies have found a way to adapt: They provide new employees exposure by assigning them special projects in addition to their regular projects. These special projects usually require the recruit to get involved in a new job function or industry. At the very least, the special projects allow recruits to appreciate aspects of the company outside their normal job duties.

If done correctly, special assignments are a win-win: The company gets another project accomplished, and the new hire gets insight into another facet of the profession. The key in this situation is to support these special projects by giving new hires the time and resources to accomplish them. Google, one of the hottest companies recruiting on campus today, allows all its engineers to spend 20 percent of their time to accomplish an independent project. It also highlights the successful products that have emerged from this program on the company blog, where computer users all over the world are asked to test them out.

3. Provide a diverse set of job responsibilities.

Sometimes a particular position will expose a new recruit to different facets of the business or industry. Start-ups have an advantage here because everyone has to pitch in on different parts of the business in the early stages. In the best situations, students design hardware for a company, meet the customer the next day to troubleshoot problems, and help the marketing department write specifications for a new product the following day.

Microsoft's program manager position may be one of the most attractive positions to new recruits because it is perceived as the jack-of-all-trades. The job allows them to develop their skills in technology and management at the same time. Again, every position and every company is different. If a particular position can be crafted so that varied exposure is built into the job itself, you have an attractive proposition for top talent.

4. Establish formal extracurricular/learning time.

If it isn't possible for you to do one of the first three, the next best thing is to formally require extracurricular/learning time. This can take many different forms. Some companies let new hires shadow another employee in another part of the company for a week. Other companies offer seminars where recruits learn about the industry overall or about other parts of the company. Some companies offer a series of lectures and networking events. Yahoo! and Google, for example, bring in renowned speakers to keep their employees informed about a variety of topics not limited to technology.

Most companies combine these options to create something that works for them. Morgan Stanley's IT division sponsors lectures and seminars for interns and new hires that are delivered by senior leadership from all over the company. Even though the new hires may be working on developing new technology solutions to support the trading businesses, they are also learning about Morgan Stanley's core business. It's a win-win for Morgan Stanley: The IT employees actually understand why they are developing the products they are, and this makes communication between them and the traders much easier. Plus, the IT employees feel as though they are being valued and exposed to the big picture.

5. Cultivate an informal work environment.

Informal environments can also encourage employees to learn about other aspects of the industry or company. Start-ups are inherently at an advantage because the work space is usually so small that new employees are constantly exposed to everything. But large companies can still foster learning across the organization, especially for interns. Johnson & Johnson encourages interns to help other groups once they have finished their own work. This gives motivated recruits the opportunity to indulge their curiosity and show valuable initiative.

ADVANCING THEIR CAREERS

Helping new hires figure out what they want to do by exposing them to different projects, industries, and job functions will make you an attractive employer. To become an ideal employer, you must also actively help your recruits advance their careers. Show today's top graduates proof that you've advanced the careers of new hires, and they'll be eager to join your team, even if it means low pay or unglamorous work.

In Wall Street trading firms, for example, interns and new hires are asked to order and pick up lunch for their more experienced colleagues on the trading desk. Very often, rounding up the grub seems like the most useful thing they do all day. It doesn't bother them a bit, though, because the firms have laid out a clear path for advancement: lunch duty for several months, then some assistant trading, then full-time trading; if they add enough value to the team they'll be raking in six-figure bonuses in only two or three years.

There's more that appeals to young recruits than money, though. The Peace Corps has enlisted thousands of new college graduates to take on very challenging work in many difficult living situations and for very little financial compensation. The Corps has proven to recruits that devoting two years to the organization not only won't limit career options but will actually enhance them. They can point to a slew of successful alumni who went on to great jobs and graduate schools—a powerful network that can boost the careers of future Peace Corps alumni.

SPEAKING OF GRADUATE SCHOOL . . .

Many of today's top graduates know they want to go to graduate school at some point, but they might not know exactly what they want to study or which school they want to attend. They do know, however, that they want to go to the best (highest-ranked) graduate school possible. So they look for employers with strong track records in propelling former employees into the top graduate programs.

Management consulting firms like McKinsey and investment banks like Goldman Sachs win this game because they seem to be the only employers broadcasting their batting averages for helping former analysts jump to top business schools. Thus, most juniors and graduating seniors at competitive colleges think the only way to get into Harvard Business School is to work in these two industries. This is simply not the case.

Whether it's business, law, medical, or engineering school your recruit has on her mind, you need to tell her explicitly that working for your organization is (a) not going to hurt her chances of being admitted and (b) going to actually improve the likelihood of her admission. You should even explain how it's possible for her to earn a graduate degree without leaving the company to do it.

MIT graduate Doug is currently working for GE Aircraft Engines. He has an interest in the aerospace industry, but what ultimately sold him on GEAE was a special program that supports graduate studies at many engineering schools, including Tufts. For Doug, earning an engineer's salary and working on real projects while getting a graduate degree is the best of both worlds.

THE NEXT BEST POSITION

Just as McKinsey boasts in its recruiting that nearly all of its entry-level hires are later admitted to top graduate school programs, McKinsey's business analyst program is also known to be a springboard to leadership positions in several different industries.

While Microsoft may not openly discuss former new hires leaving the company to take on exciting leadership positions with other organizations, its alumni do. Start-ups often advertise that their founders worked at Microsoft after graduating from college. Since many top college graduates want to start a company of their own someday, they latch onto this as proof that working at Microsoft is a good way to develop the skills and credibility to become entrepreneurs at a young age.

While making recruits feel they must make a long-term commitment is the kiss of death in college recruiting, talking about possible paths for advancement within your own organization is good for you and your prospects. You can show internal career tracks just as you show evidence of former employees moving on to awesome experiences elsewhere. Applied Materials, based in Santa Clara, California, has a rotation program that allows entry-level hires to work in different parts of the company; the rotation gives recruits great exposure and a jump-start to their careers in only 18 months. That graduates of this rotation program have about a one-third greater chance of being promoted than other employees makes Applied Materials a highly desired employer.

Openly advertising that working in your organization is a way into a great graduate school or an exciting new position will help you turn the heads of today's top college recruits. But to seal the deal and improve your chances of retaining new hires once they're on the job, you have to get specific. How is working for you going to look on their résumés? It's nice if your organization can offer them widespread name recognition, but it's actually more important that spending a couple of years with you gives them the substantive achievements and respectable responsibilities they will need to advance to the next stage of their careers, whether inside or outside of your company.

If today's top recruits can't document it, it didn't happen. They want metrics and milestones interspersed in their work experiences so they always have something to shoot for and are able to show others (grad school admissions committees, their peers, or their mothers) what they accomplished and how they were recognized. They began developing this habit in elementary school when they got star stickers on worksheets well done and their names printed in the local newspaper when they made the honor roll; they aren't about to change now. Here are five ways to demonstrate that you are advancing their careers:

1. **Award your best hires new titles and/or promotions at least once every two years.**

   The easiest way to show new hires that they are superstars—so they can communicate this to grad schools and future employers—is to offer opportunities for promotions with new titles. Wall Street investment banks like Morgan Stanley and Lehman Brothers promote their analyst-level investment banking superstars after two years. Everyone knows that if you have that senior analyst title, you were asked to stay for a third year, which means you are a superstar.

   Two years is a good rule of thumb. No opportunity for advancement within two years will not be attractive to the best students. One senior officer from a very large clothing company said that it takes five years to be promoted in the company's new-hire buyers' program. The company also happens to have a very high attrition rate (for many reasons). Five years is an eternity to this generation. If they are not given some formal title change within two years, many of the best recruits will leave or not even consider you in the first place.

2. **Give them increased or new responsibilities.**

   If you can't award a new title, then you must make sure you increase new hires' responsibilities every six months to a year. Be sure to explain that, even though they may not be getting a title change, these new responsibilities can be quantified and will help them advance their careers.

One experience that every new graduate wants, for example, is the opportunity to manage a small team or project. Top recruits realize that management experience, no matter how small, will help them learn the critical skills for smashing success inside the company—and later in their careers.

I received offers from both Bridgewater Associates [a hedge fund] and Goldman Sachs. I never thought there would be a firm that I would choose over Goldman, but my experience with Bridgewater was terrific. Once I was given the offer, the company took me and other students with offers out to dinner, brought us up to the company to visit and spend the night, and gave us a personalized tour, describing in detail what we'd be doing. What put them over the top for me was the emphasis on the responsibility I would have. They made me believe that our work would be an important asset to the company and [that we] will have the potential to go far in the company.

—David, business/economics major, Princeton University

---

3. Increase their compensation at regular intervals, especially after they successfully complete key projects.

A raise in pay is one of the easiest ways for employees to measure their career progress. Even young new hires understand that, with each pay raise, the company is making a strong statement about their professional value. They know that it is easier to convince another department or another employer to give you more money if you are already making a higher salary.

But don't stop at just awarding more money at standard intervals. Award new hires more pay after they have accomplished a key project, when they least expect it. Google uses its famed Founders' Awards to remunerate employees who make significant contributions to important projects. If new hires receive monetary awards outside the regular interval, they will always be on their toes.

4. Give them special recognition for their achievement.

Recognizing the achievements of new hires through special nonmonetary-awards programs is a great way to show them that you are actually helping them advance their careers. Companies can recognize new hires for a variety of reasons, from taking a leadership role to interacting with customers and clients to providing the team insight that was valuable.

5. Provide career coaching and direct support.

Of course new hires are looking for chic titles, awards, and increased responsibility, but at the end of the day, they also want solid coaching and advice. They look for a company to openly and honestly coach them on their career paths.

This coaching can take many forms. The standard practice of monthly one-on-one meetings works just fine most of the time. The CTO of Thomson West talks to his top interns about their careers twice a month for 45 minutes during their summer internships. The interns absolutely love it. They appreciate that someone at the company can step back and really guide them toward what may be best for them. And honest guidance like this is great for business. Thomson West continues to recruit some of the best young talent because everyone knows about this coaching culture.

Some companies take career advancement to the next level by actually helping recruits find new positions, even at another company. McKinsey supports an alumni program for all the students who complete its new-graduate business analyst program. During the recruiting process, it boasts about how well connected the recruits will be by joining the firm (even after they leave)—a key selling point for young graduates with their careers ahead of them.

✥ *Chapter Takeaway:* The first step in successful recruiting is to truly understand your potential hires—their values, their career goals, and their psychology. They have been training for their careers for a long time and are intensely aware of the importance of their first choice out of the gate. Give them a sense that your company offers open-endedness, flexibility, growth, prestige, and respect when it comes to their careers.

2

Habitually Wooed
and Gladly Dazzled

Every year we hear from many employers who want to recruit on campuses they haven't visited before. Whether young or old, small or large, organizations recruiting on a campus for the first time or returning after a hiatus (like the dot-com bust) all face the same problem. They are starting with zero presence on campus and wonder how they will attract the attention of potential applicants.

In one meeting with three representatives from just such an employer—a frontline recruiter, a hiring manager, and an executive—we asked them to describe their goals for recruiting at MIT that year.

"We only want the best ten students from this department," said the executive.

"How are you planning to attract those students?" we asked.

The frontline recruiter didn't miss a beat. "We'll have an ad running for three weeks in the student newspaper, we're hosting an information session at the end of the final week, and then we'll conduct interviews after that."

We responded, "That sounds like a fine schedule, but given that this is your first year recruiting here and your brand isn't especially familiar to our students, you might want to think about some other ways to reach your target students, like . . ."

The hiring manager interrupted, "But we're offering free pizza at our information session!"

Free pizza is the biggest cliché in college recruiting. A generation ago a couple of slices from Domino's were enough to lure students to anything. Now, with colleges increasing the quality of food on and around campus to woo students and justify hefty price tags to parents, top recruits are used to eating well. Acclaimed chefs prepare gourmet meals in Princeton eating clubs, nearly every type of cuisine at every price is within a short walk or drive of UCLA, and Emory University is famous for something like Easter brunch seven days a week. No one's going hungry. So if free pizza is the best you've got, then you've got problems.

College students are used to real competition for their attention. Born the most affluent generation ever, they grew up being marketed to by Nintendo and Sega, McDonald's and Burger King, Nike and Reebok. While they continue to make choices as consumers, these habitually wooed and gladly dazzled young people have progressed to a more serious decision: Where should I go to work?

If you want your organization's name to be their answer, you have to market to them in style. You have to give them glamour. Here's a student from the University of Illinois at Urbana-Champaign describing a classic glamour recruiting strategy: "I talked to a recruiter at about 2 P.M. on a Monday. He told me about a great opportunity with the firm and at 6 P.M. I was on a plane headed to New York for a recruiting event. We went to a penthouse in Manhattan where they had delicious food and wine. We were able to interact with partners one-on-one and really see what the company was about. Also, when we arrived, there were people already assigned to show us around and answer any questions about the interview the next day. I was truly impressed!"

But a New York gambol is not the only way to dazzle recruits.

Any new, exclusive, or flat-out *cool* experience is alluring to college students. Remember their youth and inexperience. Any seasoned professional knows that living out of a suitcase and eating room service alone at 10 P.M. isn't fun, but college students are positively giddy at the first mention of the phrase "business trip."

In this chapter, you'll learn many ways—including ones that don't cost much—to make your recruits feel special enough to want to work for you, continue working for you, and tell others to do the same.

SHOW ME THE MONEY!

It's no surprise that the finance industry has won the hearts, minds, and sign-ons of many college students simply by flashing cold, hard cash. We meet many students who dream of working on Wall Street, whether or not they have the slightest clue what jobs there entail. The reason most recruits want Wall Street? Money. Sure, at first a few give reasons like "I enjoy working with people" (as if they wouldn't work with people in any other job). When we call them on it, though, these students admit their motivation is to make as much money as fast as they can.

But the Wall Street–bound are not the only recruits who want to be rich. Of the more than 1,000 college students and recent graduates we surveyed, money was second only to the work itself among reasons people like their first-choice profession, and it was the biggest factor in why they chose their first-choice profession over their second choice. As an Ernst & Young study showed, a stunning 75 percent of college students expect to become millionaires in their lifetimes, and 30 percent believe they will be millionaires by age forty.

Thanks to financial firms like Goldman Sachs and consulting firms like McKinsey & Company, college graduates entering the workforce see $60,000 and $100,000 per year as important milestones. Recruits who enter the analyst programs typical at those companies *do* earn around $60,000 annually, and that's not counting bonuses, which in good years can be 80 to 100 percent of salary for first-year analysts at top financial firms. After two or three years' work, these entry-level analysts are either "up or out." The few who go "up" are promoted to post-MBA-level roles with annual salaries well into the six figures. And the rest move on to other organizations or to top business schools.

When students first learn of this structure of early career paths in consulting and finance, they often forget about all that initially attracted them to these industries (the work itself, the nice clothes, the jet-setting lifestyle, the $60,000 starting salary) and become totally captivated by a new dream: "I could be making six figures in my first year out of college."

In reality, depending on their majors, most college graduates make well below $60,000 as a starting salary. Engineering majors may earn as much as $50,000 on average to start, while liberal arts graduates typically start around $30,000. Thus, in addition to the starting salary you offer (which should be commensurate with peer employers in your industry and location), you should be concerned with all aspects of your recruits' probable compensation and *possible* future rewards. This includes performance raises, annual bonuses, stock options, and salary levels of positions to which they could be promoted. And if your organization can create a reward structure that gets your best and brightest to a $100,000 salary in a few years—or any offer that would be attractive to today's top recruits—you must communicate this in the recruiting process. Your compensation packages must be on par with those of your peer employers, but they must also compete with those of Microsoft, McKinsey, and Goldman Sachs. Every employer of new college graduates is competing for the same students. If you can't beat Goldman Sachs with sheer dollars, then you must be ready to win students over in other ways (we'll get to these later).

The good news is that not all students expect their first employer to dole out a $60,000 salary and a $50,000 bonus the first year. But they do expect that their next steps will put them on paths to elaborate earnings in the future. It's this mind-set that propels some students to professional schools for medicine, law, or dentistry. In other words, they are willing to take out huge loans and live off meager stipends for years because they trust that it's a path to higher earnings and more than a middle-class lifestyle when their schooling and training are completed.

Even though students give consideration to your ability to help them get rich in the future, they will not work for free. They've heard war stories of college graduates during the dot-com boom (and nongraduates who left school early) who labored for mountains of stock options with the hopes of cashing in big in a future IPO. They also know that if they're going to earn nonprofit wages, they may as well go to work for an actual nonprofit. After all, some wealthy, powerful people have started their careers in the Peace Corps.

In the end, the two rules of money in recruiting are: (1) If you've got it, flaunt it, and (2) For every bit of the top dollar you can't offer, you have to compensate in other ways—like helping recruits get into graduate school, gain experience, or develop skills that will make your organization or another one show them the money in the future.

THE ROAD ~~NOT~~ TAKEN

When Christine, an aeronautical engineering major, asked for advice on applying to work for Boeing Satellite Systems, we told her to seriously consider the company's great tuition reimbursement for graduate schools nearby in the Los Angeles area. Christine was dubious. Although she'd heard about reimbursement programs, she didn't know anyone who'd taken advantage of them. She thought there must be so many hoops to jump through to get the reimbursement that nobody actually ever did it—that it was just a marketing ploy. *Au contraire*. Juan, another student who had recently earned his master's degree from the very strong aerospace engineering department at UCLA, said Boeing not only paid for his degree, it gave him the scheduling flexibility to work, go to school, and to feel like he still had a life. When Christine heard this, her eyes lit up: "Where can I apply?"

You won't consistently win recruits with the simple promise that a stint with your organization will keep their careers on the fast track. You have to tell them stories about people who started out just like them and who, with your help, went on to reach milestones such as making a six-figure salary after X years, earning a graduate degree, or whatever else your recruits are shooting for. If they don't see evidence, they'll assume it hasn't happened. And very few students these days have the faith and audacity to be sold down the road not taken. Most prefer that you hand them a map of the road that's been taken again and again.

In the same way that Harvard sells incoming students on walking the same halls as presidents, Nobel laureates, and Fortune 500 CEOs, McKinsey touts the out-of-this-world acceptance rate of its analyst classes at elite business schools. Few organizations have track records comparable to McKinsey's, and that's okay. Christine was sold on Boeing once she heard that Juan had actually made Boeing's tuition reimbursement program work for him. Maybe your most desired recruit is itching to start his own company and would consider working for yours first if he knew about all of your former employees who went on to become entrepreneurs.

Stories of how working for you has helped people's careers should be the centerpiece of your recruiting message: *Tony's accelerated position lets him learn the many parts of our business. We paid for Juan's master's degree and made his schedule flexible so he could keep working to earn his regular salary. We helped Susan develop skills she needed to run her own company; in fact, you should give her a call to chat about it.* Include these stories prominently on your recruiting Web pages, in new-hire rotation programs, in your on-campus advertising, and in the pitches of each and every person who represents your organization to students.

WHAT ABOUT INTERNS?

You do not want to land a top intern only to see her move to another company for her next internship or for her first full-time job. How can you get star interns to return?

The number one reason interns don't return for a second summer or full-time work is their desire to get experience working in as many companies and industries as possible. They have a severe fear of commitment, but only because they think that if they stay with the same company, they'll be doing the same job for the rest of their lives. Prove them wrong. Here's how to make your star interns offers they can't refuse:

1. Give interns a leg up on their peers the next time around by allowing them to start work at an earlier date. They gain great confidence by being up-to-speed before their peers.
2. Offer a financial bonus for their return. (Yes, we're talking money again, but it costs less to retain an employee than to attract and recruit a new one.)
3. Let interns have their pick of groups in which to work the second time around.
4. Set up a special mentoring program for returning intern recruits. They'll appreciate your investing more in them.

Finally, if you're successful in your efforts to get interns to return, document the success stories as you go. If you want to consistently sell future interns on second terms or full-time employment with your organization, you need evidence that it's worked before.

GETTING INTO HARVARD—AGAIN

From vying for high school valedictorian honors to battling for orchestra first chair, new-generation college graduates are trained to compete. Even if they have no interest in attending Harvard, many of these students apply anyway just to see if they can get in. For years they've been told they're the "best and brightest," and they've relished that superlative phrase not only for the compliment to their own abilities, but also because it means they are better than everyone else.

Our popular media reflect this. Competitive reality shows like *Survivor* and *The Bachelor* rule the airwaves because of the heated rivalries among contestants who become as obsessed with ensuring others lose as they are with orchestrating the win for themselves. This was illustrated in especially dramatic fashion in the season four finale of Donald Trump's *The Apprentice*. Randal Pinkett, a thirty-four-year-old entrepreneur and former Rhodes Scholar with three MIT degrees, and Rebecca Jarvis, a recent University of Chicago graduate who had gone on to investment banking and business journalism, were the final two contestants. Randal and Rebecca had blown away the other 16 competitors, and each was a worthy and competent apprentice. Shortly after The Donald said, "You're hired!" to Randal, he asked Randal if he should also hire Rebecca. Without hesitation, Randal replied, "No. I firmly believe this is *The Apprentice*, not *The Apprenti*."

Many were shocked by how quickly Randal abandoned his previously modest, lead-by-example behavior to squabble over a TV title that the world knew he had won outright. But your top recruits weren't fazed. We polled over 40 students the next day and nearly all said that Randal did the right thing and that they would have done the same.

What does this mean for your college recruiting? The more competitive and exclusive your recruiting process is (or seems), the more attractive your organization will be to students. Here are three ways to dazzle students and make them regard your organization as the Harvard they want to apply to just to see if they can make the cut.

Create a competitive internship program

Even if you can't transform your entire college recruiting program with the flip of a switch, you *can* change one small part, as IBM did with its Extreme Blue program. Extreme Blue is a small, elite summer internship program in which undergraduate engineering majors (mostly rising seniors) are paired with MBA candidates and given the challenge of creating new minibusinesses, products, or services to address some of IBM's most pressing issues. Extreme Blue interns are mentored by celebrated IBM employees, and they get to live in the cool cities where IBM has offices (Austin, Raleigh-Durham, and San Francisco). Furthermore, the intense work experience culminates in a full day of presentations to top executives at IBM, including the CEO.

Word of IBM's prestigious Extreme Blue program has spread quickly. Other companies often grant automatic interviews to former Extreme Blue interns. Students tell us they want to work for Extreme Blue, almost completely forgetting that the company is actually IBM. And when students do become Extreme Blue interns, they never say they worked for IBM alone. They say they worked for IBM Extreme Blue to ensure everyone knows they were selected among the best of the best.

Now that college students know that Extreme Blue interns are labeled as IBM's rising stars who get their pick of just about any job at any of the company's many locations, more freshmen and sophomores are applying to intern at IBM, with hopes of improving their chances of later getting into Extreme Blue. This one internship program works wonders for IBM, inspiring noncommittal, "explore-your-options" students to *want* to return to a company that some perceive as big and boring.

Create an accelerated full-time program for rising leaders

Leadership development programs in large companies aren't as popular now as they were 15 years ago, but when executed correctly, they remain a powerful weapon in recruiting top talent and getting that talent to stay.

General Electric, for example, has a long track record of developing great leaders, starting from a young age. GE currently offers several entry-level leadership programs—in areas including finance and human resources, operations, and engineering—that enroll only the company's top new hires. Program participants attend special seminars, work on a variety of projects so they can quickly appreciate many parts of the business, receive coaching and mentoring from top guns, are explicitly put on track for promotion to meaningful positions, and form close ties with the other rising stars in their programs. They're even encouraged (with company assistance) to earn master's degrees from elite universities.

Like IBM's Extreme Blue, these leadership programs at GE attract applicants in droves because they are exclusive and high profile, and they provide established paths to amazing career opportunities. Says Jennifer Pinson, a hiring manager at GE, "These programs are the cornerstone of our recruiting process. We help train them. We help them meet other leaders internally. And this program helps us to keep our very best, as well as to attract next year's top talent."

Let them know how exclusive and competitive your recruiting program is

Why do all recruits think that companies like Microsoft are "only looking for the best" and that they traditionally extend very few offers to new hires? Because that's exactly what such organizations tell everyone. It's not enough for your recruiting to be competitive. You have to advertise that it's competitive, or no one will know. Once target recruits know that what you offer isn't so easy to get, their whole mind-set about you will change. Vijay, a Brown alumnus, recalls his Morgan Stanley recruiters bragging about how competitive it was: "They told me, 'Getting a job here is more difficult than getting into any school.'" Another student interned at a major video-game company. This intern was exceptional, so at summer's end the company asked him to return the following year. When they made the offer, they also let him know the small percentage of the company's interns that were getting an early offer to return without having to go through interviews again. They asked that he not tell anyone that number. He accepted the offer because he was so thrilled to be one of such a select group. Now, because he clearly didn't keep that percentage number a secret, more students at MIT are applying to this video-game company just to see if they can get in.

Most technology companies, however, would do well to heed that "Don't tell anyone that number" advice themselves. We've heard recruiters brag about how 80 to 90 percent of their summer interns were asked to return for internships and full-time jobs. It's one thing to tell school career offices about recruiting operations, but it could be recruiting suicide to include that in a sales pitch to students. Students have always wanted to hear about what the best can achieve, not what *anyone* can get.

DURING THE DOT-COM boom of the 1990s, a recruiter from a fast-growing Internet consulting firm bragged to a few MIT students about how he was practically giving away $55,000-a-year jobs. The incident quickly became a joke that spread like wildfire throughout the student body, and the firm's image went from exclusive to desperate faster than that recruiter could give away another job.

For today's top college graduates, getting an offer from Microsoft, McKinsey, or Google is like getting a second fat admissions envelope from Harvard. If you can create an elite internship program or an accelerated entry-level leadership program (or both), and start spreading the word about your extremely selective recruiting process, students will begin to celebrate receiving your offers, too. For young people, there's nothing more special than getting something few others have.

> Unlike the majority of firms I interviewed with, the firm I ultimately accepted an offer from didn't have a big name to flash around or a wad of cash to stick in my pocket. But what they did communicate to me amazingly well was their ability to offer me what no other investment bank could, the opportunity to build a new practice from the ground up and gain the same level of experience in two years as I would otherwise earn in four years at a firm on the Street. Whether it was divine salesmanship or not, I guess the next couple years will determine that. But did it make me accept the offer? Hell, yes.
>
> —Darren, business/economics, University of Pennsylvania

YOU CAN'T GIVE SOMETHING YOU DON'T HAVE

The cardinal rule about glamour is that you need some in order to give some. More companies are beginning to recognize the need to inject a little flash into their recruiting, but if they try without really having anything to show off, students instantly know it's just trickery.

One highly regarded recruit from Stanford notes that full-page ads in the campus newspaper didn't impress him: "We're numb to them. They all say 'amazing people, stellar projects,' but then the people aren't amazing and the projects aren't that stellar."

Glamorizing the organization is especially difficult if the company has experienced an unusually long stretch of downsizing. Morale is down and uncertainty is about the only thing that's certain. This is an unfortunate dilemma because it is during tough times that companies most need fresh talent. One struggling communications company wanted to make a comeback on a college campus. The recruiters thought they would establish an elite program for their best interns, their own version of Extreme Blue, and hoped that all employees would rally behind the new recruiting effort, supporting a strong campaign of wooing and dazzling even though the company was experiencing tough times. The program never got off the ground because the employees responsible for presenting the business units to the students could not make a compelling case for working for the company. As one recruit said, "I don't get the sense that these people actually like their jobs. They robotically recite a list of company benefits, but don't seem to like working there at all."

You need to feel special yourself before you can make others feel special. That communications company clearly didn't, but top recruiters like Microsoft and McKinsey do.

GATHER YOUR TOP GUNS

One surefire way to get the attention of target recruits (and, really, all students on a campus) is to involve your top guns: a few executives with fancy titles. We're not talking about having the CEO give a quick five-minute speech only to be whisked away and never seen by prospects again. Get a few of your biggest stars to make real contributions to your recruiting process, or create internships and entry-level jobs in which your recruits actually rub elbows with them, and students will swoon over your organization.

One student was on the fence about working for a prestigious investment bank, but when the vice chairman of the board called him, he was instantly sold. He could not stop talking about how cool it was to receive a call from the vice chairman. It was evident that he didn't really get to know Mr. Vice Chairman, nor did he know what a vice chairman really does, but that didn't matter. What mattered was getting that call.

Students are even more impressed when companies send senior people to interview them on campus. Apple often sends executives to interview potential interns, and students report being "blown away." One student asked an Apple executive why he had come, only to be told, "Recruiting, and especially recruiting college hires, is among my most important tasks." Other companies are as surprised by this as the students. Several say they just don't understand how Apple's executives make the time. Maybe they just "think different." Maybe you should, too.

During the interview process with Promontory Financial Group, I interviewed with Eugene Ludwig, Promontory's CEO and former U.S. comptroller of the currency. This really amazed me, both because of his extensive banking expertise and also because of how genuinely personable and enthusiastic he was. I left the interview really wanting to work for the firm.

—Caroline, business/economics, Princeton University

Although big titles always wow students, sometimes your best big-shot recruiters can be recent hires. Consulting firms are great at using this tactic. At on-campus information sessions and career fairs to recruit the next entry-level analyst class, some firms showcase a handful of people from their last entry-level analyst class who have been promoted faster than their peers or have made some unique impact in the firm. Have an executive tell the crowd of students how lucky the firm is to have hired Susan because she's doing great work on such and such project, and BAM! You've created a superstar in the eyes of the students—one with a level of success to aspire to, and someone who will have some serious pull with your target recruits.

Also remember: You have a lot more entry-level people than top executives, and their time is less valuable to your organization. Get these public endorsements right and you engender an army of top-gun recruiters.

Sometimes a junior person doesn't even need to have proven that he is a rising star in your organization before becoming very useful to you. On just about every campus, there are several students who are revered most highly by everyone in the school. They run the high-profile student groups, they win the big awards, they have professors in their back pockets, and they land the most sought-after jobs. Last year's senior hero-gods have sway and influence well beyond graduation. So take them with you when recruiting at their alma maters.

After speaking with only three students at Georgia Tech, we discovered a common short list of top guns from the previous year's graduating class. It was clear that these three students would be in awe if they were recruited by these graduates and excited about following in their footsteps. Employers of those former campus leaders could have easily used them as a competitive advantage in recruiting.

LOW-COST WAYS TO GLAM UP YOUR RECRUITING ACT

Most employers don't think they can recruit with glamour because they "just don't have the money." We won't lie—having money certainly makes things easier. At Princeton, one career office staff member told us that employers are likely to attract more students when they pay to hold information sessions at a nearby hotel rather than in the classrooms they can use for free. "Students like getting dressed up and eating cheese and crackers," she noted. "They think it's more professional and classy, even if it's just across the street."

Still, there are plenty of low-cost things you can do to wow the recruits you want. In fact, some of the most effective tactics barely cost anything:

1. **Mail recruits a copy of your CEO's book.**

    If your CEO has written a book or there has been a book written about your company, dress it up further with an autograph. If your leader isn't such a prolific writer and your organization isn't a media darling, send a book about a big idea relevant to the future of your business or any other book that one of your leaders has found to be especially inspirational. This shows your recruits that you believe they, too, can be thought leaders for your company someday.

2. **Send a good-luck e-mail on final exam day.**

    Better yet, send a care package with popcorn, chocolate, and a Starbucks gift certificate.

3. **Go off the record.**

    Have one of your employees who is a recent graduate from the school take your recruit out to lunch. Make the conversation officially off the record so the recruit can discuss the real job without feeling pressure. Students love transparency.

4. **Use your powerful alumni network.**

    Go beyond telling stories of what previous employees of your company have gone on to do. Arrange for your recruits to talk to them by phone or in person.

5. **Offer new recruits something they consider a luxury item.**

It could be a monthly one-hour massage, which they'd ordinarily never get. For others, quarterly tickets to a sports event can help clinch the deal. What costs you a little can go a long way with the right audience. What works best? Is it more training? A monthly lunch with a senior executive? Understand your recruits and offer them something they can enjoy (and tell their friends about).

6. **Go backstage.**

During the interview, take your recruits where people normally aren't allowed. If we were Intel, for example, all of us would be putting on bunny suits and going in the clean rooms. Give students something to talk about.

IMPORTANT, INDISPENSABLE, AND IN EVERYONE'S INBOX

One key to getting your interns to return and entry-level hires to stay is to work their butts off. We asked top students whether they preferred a nine-to-five job with reasonably important work or twelve-hour days in the thick of things, and nine out of ten said they preferred the latter. That's an astonishing finding—and it's common among top recruits. Very often the most talented college graduates choose to work for consulting firms or investment banks over, say, a Fortune 500 manufacturing company simply because they want a more intense experience. In fact, Microsoft is one of the few employers outside the fields of consulting and finance that has been able to glamorize its actual work by making it intense and important. Here's what Microsoft does, and what you can, too.

Make interns (temporarily) indispensable

Sure, just about every employer tells us that their interns and entry-level hires do "real" work and not just busywork. Yet the first complaints from interns and new hires are always about not having work that matters and not really being needed. It's not enough to put your new hires on projects that *you* think matter; you have to be sure the work matters to your employees. You may even have to crunch the due dates to create some urgency, spell out the importance for them, and consistently remind them of how much their contributions mean to the organization.

One rule of thumb is a simple question of great importance to an intern: If she were gone for more than a couple of days, would her colleagues notice? (Maybe you should even use this question to test whether *you* are indispensable!) If after an absence nobody even noticed that you were gone or it didn't negatively affect the outcome of your projects, then you're not really adding that much value in the first place. And that's the last thing your recruits want to feel.

Real work is one area in which start-ups have a huge inherent competitive advantage. A start-up doesn't have the financial or human resources to put someone on the payroll just to do busywork—not even a student. Post–summer internship evaluations consistently show that students who work at start-ups report being more satisfied with their internships than their Fortune 500 counterparts because they feel needed at work.

If your company is located 20 miles west of Detroit, and your headquarters are more warehouse than designer office space, you might think it's a tall order to create glamour for recruits. But the small robotics company Shafi Inc. did it with flying colors. Shafi brought in a sophomore from MIT to do software and mechanical work one summer. After having the intern shadow a full-time engineer for a couple of weeks, the company gave him more and more responsibility as he proved himself on the job. Eventually, he owned his own project, which required him to interact directly with customers and suppliers. He even traveled to a customer site, and his work was so impressive the customer offered him contract work in addition to his internship with Shafi. The intern certainly loved the work he tackled by day, but he became even more enthralled with Shafi by night, when he spoke with friends interning all over the country. Hearing how his friends' employers limited them to bite-sized pieces of projects made him think his internship was the hottest ever. He knew he was getting an opportunity none of his friends could imagine.

Let them talk with customers

Shafi did more than make that intern feel indispensable by giving him full responsibility for his own project. They also let him interact directly with customers. This may not seem like a big deal to you, but to an intern it's monumental. Putting your recruit at the service of customers either internal or external is another easy way to make him feel needed.

Not every situation warrants having a new hire or intern work closely with customers. In fact, it may not even be appropriate at times, but that doesn't mean you shouldn't look for similar interactive communication opportunities for your recruits. Indirect customer contact can also prove to students that their work matters. After his junior year, Ian interned at IncTank, an early-stage venture capital firm in Cambridge, Massachusetts. Ian's manager frequently asked him to sit as a silent participant in important conference calls and face-to-face meetings. Even though most of his work was unrelated, Ian felt like a real member of the team and not some back-office data robot because he was privy to important conversations and was frequently asked for his opinion.

Give them the chance to achieve something tangible

Companies that actually make products or provide tangible services—as opposed to simply advising or consulting—have a real advantage here, but every employer can provide opportunities for new hires to rack up the following:

1. Patents

This is a no-brainer for engineering and technology companies. A patent is validation of an engineer's innovation and creativity. Every college graduate knows that having patents in your name gives you excellent credibility and helps you get into graduate school or land a better job. Still, very few companies inform their recruits of the potential for earning patents while working for their organization or even the glory that comes with receiving them. If you don't celebrate new patent holders, start now!

2. Publications

Whether it's a blurb on your organization's Web site or a longer work printed in a peer-reviewed industry or academic journal, a piece of writing with your name on it is big for building your personal brand early in a career. Students know that published writing is universally respected and will afford them a bit of fame and a leg up on others for future job or graduate school applications. (And it will look as great on their résumé as on their mother's refrigerator!)

3. Speaking engagements

Speaking at industry conferences or even at important internal events gives young talent similar benefits: name recognition and credibility that go a long way to boosting careers and self-esteem.

4. Special awards

Though awards vary by organization, one rule holds true for all: The more well-known the award is, the better. It doesn't matter if you recognize individual performance or team performance. What matters is that you establish special awards programs and celebrate them. Most important, make sure your target recruits know about them. And take them seriously yourself. If it isn't meaningful enough to brag about to peers, parents, or future employers, it's not worth a thing to recruits.

5. Publicity

Your target recruits are used to achieving recognition and having their names published in local newspapers, such as when they made the honor roll or the National Honor Society. So play to their vanity and publicize their projects, patents, presentations, and awards anywhere you can. The bigger and more public, the better, but your organization's Web site or company e-mail newsletter is also a place to start. The most important thing is for the recruit to know others can see his accomplishments.

While I was interning at Microsoft, a senior VP took the time to meet me and later wrote an entry in his public blog about my project. Surely this wasn't intended to be a recruiting gesture, but one of the effects was that I felt a connection to an important manager, and this had a positive influence when I considered Microsoft for a full-time position.

—Jared, grad student, science/engineering, MIT

COOL CITY, CULTURE, AND CLASSMATES

Big cities with lots to do—a music scene, sporting events, and a booming nightlife—are very attractive to college students deciding

where to work after college. The most popular locales for top recruits won't come as a surprise:

1. New York, especially for finance
2. San Francisco Bay Area, especially for start-ups and technology
3. Los Angeles, especially for defense or entertainment
4. Boston
5. Chicago
6. Washington, D.C.

Your target recruits might not have visited these cities or know
much about them, but they still want to work there because of the
glamour associated with them. While employers with offices in these
cities have an advantage, companies based outside these meccas can
compete, too. You just need to sell the locale as enthusiastically as
the job. The secret to this is understanding that, more than seeing
the bright lights of big cities, being around lots of other young people is what new college graduates really want. Procter & Gamble,
for example, successfully recruits top candidates to its Cincinnati
headquarters.

In college there's a seemingly endless supply of people the same
age and opportunities for fun and recreation. Students are stimu-
lated 24/7 because they can always find someone in their residence
hall, fraternity, or sorority to hang out with. The prospect of leaving
a place where everyone knows your name and moving to an entirely
new city is daunting. To give a recruit the courage to do so, you must
convince her that she won't be bored and alone in her new home-
town.

Certainly, if you catch a recruit who grew up or went to college in
the city you're recruiting for, there's a good chance he will start his
career there because the place is familiar and comes with a ready-
made network of friends. Peter, a graduate of William Jewell College

near Kansas City who went to work for a golf company near Los Angeles, is ready to switch professions just to move back to his college town: "I hate where I live because I don't know anyone here. At this point I'd be willing to take almost any type of job in Kansas City because I have friends there who tell me it's like being in college again with so many people from school around. Besides, I already know the city and I'm comfortable there."

Unfortunately, since most employers recruit outside their cities and because many top colleges are scattered across the country, keeping every new hire at home is impossible—and is hardly the point. But it really becomes each employer's responsibility to support the social lives of new hires as much as their work lives. As Emily Meehan reported in her March 3, 2006, *Wall Street Journal* article "Getting Ahead Often Means Moving Away": "Twentysomethings often lack the professional networks and the experience to strategically locate themselves and their careers in places where they also want to live."

Let the young sell the young

When you are courting recruits, make sure they meet as many young people in your organization as possible. Professional services firms like McKinsey and Goldman Sachs excel at putting prospective hires in touch with their youngest employees. The firms sponsor many lunches and other informal gatherings on college campuses where junior employees join recruiters in meeting students. It gives the students a safe place to ask the important questions about life outside work that they wouldn't dare ask in interviews with more senior people for fear of being labeled as unfocused and unprofessional.

Remember that the setting doesn't matter as much as the people. One entry-level recruit remembers a visit to Exxon at which all the young employees were invited to a lunch in the company cafeteria. It wasn't fancy, but since the recruit didn't know a soul in Texas, he really appreciated the chance to see that Exxon actually had young employees.

Dare to be different

The Boston Consulting Group (BCG) may have a great brand name on campuses across the country, but it's still not easy for them to attract new hires to cities not on our top six list. BCG's Dallas office extended full-time offers to two MIT students, Brian and Elizabeth. Dallas, of course, is a relatively large city with a vibrant young community and lots to do. Elizabeth hails from Texas, so she was the easier sell. But Brian grew up in Virginia, went to college in Boston, and had never been to Texas.

Part of the Dallas team, including all employees under age twenty-six, took Brian and Elizabeth to a barbecue dinner at a nice restaurant, in typical recruiting fashion. But the next move was unexpected: They went to a rodeo. The Texas BBQ, the opportunity to hear the young BCG employees talk about weekend parties and outings, and the chance to start friendships with the other prospective hires attending the "sell weekend" ultimately convinced both Elizabeth and Brian to accept. Said Brian, "BCG went out of its way to make me feel comfortable, connect me with young employees, and show me that Dallas is a fun city. I'm not afraid of moving to Dallas anymore, even though I don't know too many people there."

Share the burden

Knowing how tough it is to attract people to one of the coldest parts of the country, several companies in Minneapolis have joined forces to win top talent for internships and entry-level jobs. This recruiting coalition cohosts professional development events and social events for interns and new hires to highlight the many entertaining activities the Twin Cities have to offer and to connect them to the larger population of young people. It's especially effective with summer interns because the more friends they make in the area, the more likely they are to accept offers to return for full-time work. Will, an MIT student who interned at Thomson West, a company that participates in the joint initiative, said, "Before the summer, I had no idea Minneapolis could be this fun or that there were so many young people in the area."

Don't stop after the sell

Rob, who went to work for Boeing in Los Angeles after attending college in Florida, said, "When I moved to Los Angeles, I only knew three people there. And I didn't like two of them. If it hadn't been for the young professionals' social network I joined at work, I might have left as soon as I got here."

Young, a UC Berkeley grad, works in the Intuit Rotational Development Program, a newly formed leadership program for top recruits. Intuit knows the importance of getting new hires to bond early. Members of the Rotational Development Program went to Tucson for three months to work together. Said Young: "Everyone lived together, commuted together, and it was a great way to get to know my peers. Intuit paid for our housing, and every weekend we had some sort of event planned (like horseback riding). We had a peer group of 12, so we got to know everyone. We'll probably be long-term connections for the future."

Tony, a recent Goldman Sachs hire, said, "Training is a blast! I know so many people now to hang out with outside of work. It's also a great network to help me when I have a problem on the job." And that's exactly what next year's recruits will want to hear.

COOL PERKS, AND NOT JUST T-SHIRTS

Besides support for your recruits' social lives, you can also win by offering a great quality of life *at* work. Google is the current undisputed champ of creating a cool culture and community on the job because of a laundry list of perks (including on-site laundry facilities). Being a Googler, as Google employees are called, means getting all meals free and prepared on-site by gourmet chefs; all the snacks you want; free use of swimming pools, pool tables, and volleyball courts; and (in some locations) even a free ride to work on a bus equipped with wireless Internet. When prospective recruits visit Google headquarters in Mountain View, California, they realize they are going to work very hard at Google, but with all those perks, they know they'll have fun doing it.

Consider the following to make your recruits feel special:

1. Good free food

Any programming student will tell you that the baseline for food has gone up. It used to be bottled water. Now, every programmer *expects* his choice of soft drinks and energy drinks. It's a given because programmers work for hours at a computer. Give some thought to what would delight your employees. If they're working in cubicles all day during the summer, how about an outdoor break for ice cream sundaes every Friday? Whatever the food opportunities are, be sure your recruits know about them.

2. Your own products or services

If your company makes cool products or provides valuable consumer services, offer them to your recruits at no charge or at a generous discount. Bose and Apple attract students with great employee discounts on the latest multimedia gadgets. Software companies know very well that many of their young employees buy their software at hugely discounted prices and give it to friends. The companies know that each gift is a marketing opportunity for the company. College students who work at Johnson & Johnson love the discount they get on small consumer products, and retail employees trumpet their perks of discounted clothing. If you're an auto company and it's not realistic to give away your products or discount them steeply, at least allow employees to test-drive prototypes and concept vehicles.

3. Field trips

Travel is extremely glamorous—to new college grads, at least. Even if travel isn't built into the day-to-day jobs of your employees, as it is in an industry like consulting, you should mention any possible travel your new hires might do. Your recruits want to know about any chance they'll have to leave the office and meet colleagues from elsewhere, even if it's just once a year in another city in the United States. Of course, international travel has more cachet. Gemini Consulting recruiters always mentioned the firm's mandatory, two-week orientation in London or Paris as much as possible, and it absolutely helped close recruits. One Boston University student received an offer from Macquarie, an Australian-based investment bank that is expanding its operations in the United States. He wasn't excited about going into banking, but he seemed to quickly forget that detail every time he mentioned the training held in Sydney, Australia.

4. International assignments

As glamorous as a quick trip can be, the opportunity to have a short assignment abroad is even better. In our increasingly global economy, study- and work-abroad opportunities are definitely in vogue. Infosys, the India-based software company, offers an opportunity for United States–based employees to live in India for almost a year. A few years ago India wouldn't have seemed glamorous to most students, but things have changed; we have urged Infosys to make this a key selling point to their new recruits. Investment banks and consulting firms sometimes allow their best analysts to work in a foreign office for a year before applying to graduate school as an incentive for them to stay with the company longer.

5. Backstage access

We all feel cool to be in the know when others aren't. The allure of seeing things that most people don't know exist is what keeps jobs with the NSA or CIA on students' radars. One top MIT student chose Bose over several companies in his top-choice industry as soon as he learned that the project they planned for him was "top secret." One student we interviewed who had worked at a gaming company repeatedly mentioned that Sean Connery had visited his office a few times. Even though the student didn't meet the famous actor, he sure felt special just knowing that Mr. Connery had been on the premises. And backstage access isn't limited to government- or Hollywood-related jobs. Consulting firms like McKinsey sell top recruits on its access to very high-level executives at client companies and the opportunity to tell these industry giants, probably 30 years their senior, what to do with their companies. To a twenty-two-year-old, that's pretty special.

6. Cool parties and social events

Today's top recruits have long been sold on the phrase "Work hard, play hard." And boy, do they like to play. A few years ago, when the consultancy Bain & Company was recruiting new analysts, they talked up two past events that had students buzzing: a soccer tournament modeled after the World Cup that united employees around the globe, and a party on Cape Cod, at which the new class of consultants performed a hilarious skit for the entire staff of the Boston office. Bain employees even showed a video of this off-site party to make it clear to students that the party they threw was better than any college frat scene.

UNCLE SAM HAD IT RIGHT

For all the money you shower on recruits, the care you use in crafting their fast-track career paths, the competitive screening you put them through, the top guns you sic on them, the mission-critical work you let them do, and the friends and fun you make sure they enjoy, the ultimate message you need to send top college graduates is very simple: "I want YOU!" Yes, Uncle Sam's very own famed recruiting phrase.

> A company heard about the research I do and contacted me to encourage me to apply for a summer internship with them. I had already committed to doing research on campus with my advisor over the summer, so the company then contacted and came out to meet with my advisor to convince him to allow me to consult for them over the summer. They were so persistent and made me feel so valuable that I was ecstatic when my advisor agreed that I could consult for them.
>
> —John, grad student, science/engineering, Stanford University

One of the most effective ways to relay the "I want YOU" sentiment to your target recruits is to contact them personally before they even apply to work for you. Whether it is by phone or e-mail, you will pique the interest of even the most highly desired recruits. Why? "Being contacted by a company makes us feel special," explained Lisa, a senior at Georgia Tech.

Julian, a top MIT student, received an e-mail from a recruiter at

D.E. Shaw. The recruiter had found Julian's résumé on a public database and said that she would like him to apply formally for one of Shaw's job postings. The message also provided information about D.E. Shaw and the job that seemed to fit his background best. Within five minutes, Julian sent our office a frantic e-mail asking us to review his résumé "ASAP" so he could get it to the recruiter by the end of the night. We congratulated him and when we asked what was the rush, Julian replied, "No company has ever contacted me like this before, so I really want to act quickly."

Personal contact should go beyond soliciting applications and should be extended throughout your recruiting process. The recruiting team at Gemini Consulting, for example, frequently made brief phone calls to students who had been offered positions at the firm. In addition to congratulating the recruits, the calls were used to remind students what Gemini had to offer and, in particular, why Gemini wanted them. A majority of candidates accepted Gemini's offers and students reported that the phone calls made Gemini seem classier and more genuinely interested in the recruits than other firms. Even the few people who turned down offers noted that Gemini's reaching out to recruits made decision-making harder for the students.

One of the main reasons I chose to work for McKinsey was that I felt like the members of the firm, both recruiters and consultants, made a point of getting to know me personally. Throughout the recruiting process, the firm members who contacted me were matched to me based on background and interests. When the new hires arrived for a sell weekend, each of us received a personalized gift box in our hotel rooms. While other firms sent generic gifts, McKinsey gave items tailored to individuals such as a hiking trail guide for an outdoor enthusiast and a set of CDs from the city's orchestra for a classical musician.

—Mark, humanities, University of Virginia

The most direct way to say "I want YOU!" to students is to tell them explicitly that you think they're special and that you really want them to join your organization. This is one of the most underestimated and underused recruiting tactics of all. Students are inexperienced professionally, and their skills and knowledge have not been tested in the real world. Naturally, they have some self-doubt and as

---

One of my first job interviews was for a contractor position at IBM. The guy I met with did a few great things:

1. He sat me down and told me about the project. He was frank about the problems he'd run into trying to put together a team for the project. This was cool. He was obviously a very intelligent guy, but he was also surprisingly honest: "Hey, man, here's why this has been hard for us and why we need to bring in some people so we can get this done right." It made me think, *Hey, you are smart and want to get things done. You don't mind admitting difficulties or explaining them to a new guy who's obviously not as experienced as you.*

2. He asked, How would you handle this problem? He seemed to be honestly looking for ideas. How would you do *my* job, not just the one you're interviewing for?

3. He actually checked out my résumé. I had listed a freelance writing position I'd had as a soccer writer for the *Mumbai Midday,* and he said, "Yeah? Let's Google around and read some of your stuff." I'd actually never done that myself. But we found some. And he asked real questions about my job there. It made me understand he was a thorough and curious guy.

4. He took me for a walk around the company, and told me the good things and bad things about working there. I'd had these goofball interviews where people talked about how superbadass their company was, and it sounded fake. This dude was real.

—Saleem, humanities, University of North Carolina

a result will gravitate toward employers that can provide some reassurance of their value. Organizations that affirm and reaffirm their recruits' abilities and potential gain an advantage. Kofi, a chemistry graduate from Harvard, remembers one of his best experiences with a company: "My manager asked me what I wanted to do with my career. I told him, and he described how he'd help guide me and how I could transition into different areas of the company. Other coworkers spoke highly of him and I learned he was a straight shooter, someone who helped people achieve their goals."

Employers will all have different ways of glamorizing their jobs, and there are infinite possibilities—from lavish jet-setting and fine dining to the more mundane perk of discount Band-Aids to presenting very practical scenarios of possible career paths. But what your target recruits want most is for you to want them.

✤ *Chapter Takeaway:* The next most important thing to your target recruits after believing that you care about their careers is feeling that working for you includes a "cool" factor. Decide what's best given your organization's line of business, location, and budget, and make sure recruits know what you're doing for them. Only one question determines whether your "glamour" tactics work: Does it make your recruits feel special and wanted?

3

Gossip Hounds and Constant Communicators

AMS Consulting was growing rapidly, and like most firms in its industry, it needed to hire a slew of entry-level analysts to deliver on all the projects it was selling. To maximize exposure and foot traffic at the MIT Fall Career Fair, the firm paid more than $10,000 to be a platinum sponsor, which allowed it to place its booth where students would enter and exit the building. Whenever AMS recruiters liked the students who stopped by, they invited the students to a "private" casino-night party to be held that evening at Top of the Hub, a swanky fifty-second-floor restaurant and bar with a breathtaking view of Boston.

But is anything ever really "private" among college students? A couple of hours later, the party details had been forwarded by e-mail to almost every student mailing list on campus. The entire senior class was buzzing about AMS's casino-night party, and the chatter worked wonders for the firm's reputation. While AMS was previously thought to be just another technical consulting firm, that night it was as flashy and hip as Bain or The Boston Consulting Group.

Whether AMS actually intended the party to be exclusive or it was labeled "private" just to make it seem cool so students would spread the word, the gossip it generated was hugely beneficial. In an important way, the e-mails that spread for free ultimately were worth as much as the expensive career fair sponsorship and the party combined. That it was the subject of this intense chatter doubled the party's value, and it had an echo effect the following year as students remembered the buzz and talked about it again the next recruiting season.

But gossip can also be destructive. Tom wanted nothing more than to intern at a certain booming e-commerce company his sophomore year. He talked about it constantly with his professors, with staff in the career office, even with alumni. Then he applied through the standard online channel and was immediately chosen for an interview. No one was surprised; Tom had more relevant experience than any other sophomore and he had a genuine interest in the company. He aced the first interview. Second and final rounds were no different, and Tom breezed through with flying colors. He excitedly told everyone that the only thing remaining was to wait for his offer.

But Tom never received the offer. Instead, he got an e-mail from the company's recruiter stating that the company could not make him an offer because he was a sophomore and they hired only juniors for internships. In disbelief, Tom appealed to the recruiter, explaining that he had clearly indicated his sophomore status on his résumé, that he had passed three interview rounds, and that at no time had any one seemed concerned about his age. The recruiter didn't budge. It was policy.

But soon everyone on campus would know the policy. Shocked and annoyed on his behalf, the other students offered Tom condolences and wondered aloud why the company wouldn't make an exception. Intern placement staff called the recruiter to appeal once more on Tom's behalf, but the recruiter's response was simple: *No. Have him apply next year.* When the recruiter wasn't the least bit apologetic, the university staffer got upset too, and became less eager to help the company scout talent.

In later recruiting seasons, students who once thought this same company was the be-all-and-end-all didn't bother to apply. Remarkably, Tom *still* wanted to work for the firm, but dozens of other students who formerly had expressed interest in the company were so turned off by Tom's unfortunate rejection that they didn't bother to apply in subsequent recruiting seasons.

What might this employer have done differently? First, as soon as they caught the mistake, they should have apologized to Tom—in person: *We hire only juniors, and somehow we didn't notice that you're a sophomore. We messed up and we apologize.* Second, this could have been a golden moment if the company had set aside the P-word—policy. Breaking with policy isn't always possible, but when it is, bending the rules is a powerful recruiting tactic that creates a bond of loyalty.

Over 81 percent of students we surveyed said that they are "very likely" or "likely" to share their negative recruiting experiences with friends. This new generation of students spends more time talking to each other than any previous generation. And in-person gossiping is only part of it. The technologies of e-mail, instant messaging, text messaging, blogs, and online forums have enabled us to spread messages faster and wider than ever before, and young people exercise this ability to its fullest extent. At colleges where the social networking Web site Facebook.com is available, 85 percent of students are registered Facebook users, and 60 percent of them sign on daily to swap messages, share photos, and update friends on their whereabouts. Given this obsession with being in touch, it's no wonder that when one student has an interesting experience—positive or negative—with an employer, it's not long before dozens or hundreds of others hear about it.

College students are tireless when it comes to talking about their own experiences, spreading opinions, and keeping each other appraised of what's hot and what's not. And they always, always ask around about a company before accepting an offer of employment, or even an interview. Whether you like it or not, this is one of the rules of the game when recruiting or, really, doing anything involving college students. In this chapter we'll tell you what recruiting issues students buzz about most and then help prepare you to minimize the risk of negative gossip and maximize the potential for positive vibes about your organization spreading through campus.

THE TOP NINE RECRUITING ISSUES STUDENTS LOVE TO DISH ABOUT

Recruits talk about everything. They're vetting you as much as you are them, so everything is fair game—the good, the bad, and even the outrageously ugly.

1. Money

Surprise, surprise. Whenever poor college students trade the tuition bills of the academic year for the big paychecks of summer or postgraduation, they love to tell other students how much money they make. Wall Street jobs are a prime example. Each year, first-year full-time analysts return to college campuses and tell their younger friends about their year-end bonuses of tens of thousands of dollars, and soon the entire campus knows. When one of the investment banks recently raised its starting salary for first-year analysts by $5,000, word spread so fast that the other banks followed suit within a week.

2. Perks

College students and recent grads love to talk about how awesome it was that their employers sent them to Europe to meet with clients. One Apple intern bragged about getting to fly business class to China for a project—a plum perk the school's placement staff promptly shared with other students. Cool parties, great free food, and access get people chattering and excited, too.

Charlie, a sophomore economics major, interned in the PGA Tour's branding division. He liked his day job, but even better was getting to play golf after work on the famous courses at TPC Sawgrass, where The Players Championship is held each year. After hearing about Charlie's experiences, his friends and acquaintances are applying to the same internship, even though it pays less than most nonprofit gigs.

Perks don't always have to be extravagant to get talked about. Taking a recruit to a nice restaurant or sending a "Good luck on finals!" monster basket of brownies can go a long way.

3. Powerful people

When upstart Advanced Electron Beams sent its CEO to an informal networking luncheon at MIT for professionals and students, there was no need to make a formal announcement of his attendance. Within 15 minutes, students were approaching the event organizers asking where he was. "That's awesome that their CEO is here," one student said. A month later, Advanced Electron Beams posted a summer internship position and quickly received dozens of applications.

4. Competition and desperation

When asked why they want to work for particular companies, students love to talk about how cutthroat the competition is. We often hear lines like the following: "Blackstone is only taking a few students from Harvard and Wharton." "I want to work at a hedge fund because they're more prestigious." "Venture capital firms hardly ever hire." When students get word of especially competitive application processes or selective recognition programs, they want to apply just to see if they can get an offer. The flip side is that students are also likely to talk about a company in a bad way if they sense the company is desperate for hires. One recent MIT grad interviewed with a start-up and had several bad impressions throughout the recruiting process:

- The interview took place in a diner that was completely empty and in the middle of nowhere.
- The interviewer didn't know the recruit's name and spent the interview looking at the wrong résumé.
- The recruiter actually said, "The sooner you start, the more money you'll make." This was his pitch.
- He asked no technical questions or anything regarding the recruit's previous professional experience.

The recruit told friends afterward never to work for that start-up.

5. The work

One large automaker hired five summer interns through a program with which the automaker had a long-standing relationship. But when four of those interns had bad experiences and spread the word all over campus that they didn't have anything interesting to do and didn't learn anything, the company had trouble recruiting the following year and pulled out of the internship program altogether.

If the work is challenging, the results can be quite different. When the Mikva Challenge, a nonprofit in Chicago that educates young people about careers in public policy, hired Princeton grad Stephanie and put her in charge of 100 high school girls and 500 alumni right from the beginning, she excitedly told others about the responsibility. The following year a friend of Stephanie's applied to the same fellowship that placed Stephanie with the Mikva Challenge.

6. **Execution of the recruiting process**

This is the aspect of recruiting that draws by far the most complaints among recruits—and presents a big opportunity for your organization to shine. If you get it right, students will sing your praises to everyone they know. If you are not courteous and if you mismanage expectations, students will let the rest of the campus know. Recruits hate it when employers don't call when they say they will or don't extend offers until weeks after the previously discussed deadlines. Forty-five percent of students surveyed were bothered by employers not getting back to them on time. What could be simpler?

Employers who pay attention to detail leave students—even rejected ones—telling others to apply, saying, "They really had their act together," and, "Their process was really smooth." Recruits can handle less money—and even rejection—if they've heard good things about the company's recruiting practices. One Stanford graduate interviewing with Boston Consulting Group knew his interview was going badly. While trying to solve a brainteaser puzzle, he just couldn't get the numbers to work, but the interviewer remained positive and helped the student through a few steps to arrive at an answer. The recruit later found out that his interview took half as long as everybody else's. The recruiter had shortened the interview so as not to embarrass the student anymore. This uncommon compassion made the student want to work for BCG even more.

One student remembers Microsoft's attention to detail: "What impressed me wasn't just that they arranged my airfare to Redmond, or worked around my schedule, or coordinated all of my logistics (including paying for everything). On my last day, they told me that all of my charges would be taken care of, but if I had any miscellaneous reimbursements to send in, I could. Then they handed me an envelope that was stamped and preaddressed—with both Microsoft's address *and my own*. They actually dug up my address and wrote it in the corner."

Employers who don't pay attention to recruiting practice details give students something to talk about, too. And you don't want that. Kumar was interviewing for a development position with an incredibly selective technology innovation company. The preliminary phone interview was to be at noon, but the interviewer never called. Two days later, after leaving polite e-mail and phone messages inquiring when he might hear back from them, Kumar was contacted and told that his interviewer had simply forgotten. Needless to say, Kumar was disgusted.

The recruiter just seemed unprofessional. He did not take the time to even try to pronounce my name correctly, and he was also not prepared. To me, that was a bad sign and a deal breaker . . . and I warned my friends.

—Hyun, science/engineering, MIT

I was interviewing with a publishing company and they were so nice at first. Then they made an offer for a job I hadn't even interviewed for. It was for data entry, menial work! I called back when they told me to, but they weren't there. When they finally made me an offer, they couldn't provide any details. I felt like they were avoiding my questions, and yet they still wanted me to accept this vague offer. Finally, I decided I couldn't work for an organization like that one, and I stopped trying to get in touch with them.

—Angilee, English/cognitive science, University of California at Berkeley

7. The culture

It's either cool, okay, or *Office Space* (the 1999 movie about life in a stale office environment). Here's what one engineering student wrote about his experience interning at an aircraft engine plant, where the average employee age was fifty-two: "This place is worse than *Office Space*. People just stare at the computer screen and don't actually talk to one another. There is no energy and their idea of a company social is a brown-bag lunch to hear one of the engineers talk in monotone about his project—with Microsoft Project printouts. I can't wait to leave and tell everyone how bad this was."

Culture matters. Your college recruits have been living, eating, and working alongside other young people for four years. Integrate new hires and especially interns with young people in your company by setting up lunches and informal meetings. Ask your other young employees for their ideas on what *they* would want to see. Then give them a small budget and let them organize the gatherings.

8. Special treatment

When Matt interned at West, the legal information provider owned by Thomson Corporation, the chief technology officer quickly recognized that he was one of the most gifted recruits the company had ever had. This CTO met with Matt once a week just to talk and to make sure he worked on his choice of projects. When Matt was deciding what to do the following year, he was torn. He wanted a new work experience, but he knew he would have a great time at West because they proved they would look out for him, and he had developed great relationships there, including a personal friendship with the CTO. The CTO had a candid conversation with Matt about his professional goals and fears about returning to the same company.

When he learned that Matt's two biggest desires were to experience another part of the industry and to live in another part of the country, the CTO worked with human resources and other staff within Thomson, West's parent company, to arrange a position for Matt in another Thomson company's office in California. Matt took the second internship and is still telling people how impressed and grateful he was because of the way West and the Thomson Corporation treated him.

9. The outrageously ugly

Some recruiting horror stories float around the halls for years. The damage they cause for companies can be catastrophic—not only because what happened is so unbelievably bad, but because students spread the word with a vengeance, almost as if they are on a crusade. Students who hear these stories think hard before applying to the offending employers and scrutinize every move those employers make. Harassment and ridicule in an interview count in this category. So do rescinded offers. One junior at the University of Pennsylvania was shocked during his first-round interview with an investment bank. When the student began to talk about his background and interests (which were admittedly academic), the interviewers openly laughed at him. Their rudeness made a big impression on the recruit, and he told everyone how that company had made him feel.

Andrew, a Stanford engineering graduate, interviewed twice for two different positions with a large Internet company based in Silicon Valley. The interview process took four rounds and a little over three months. This was exasperating, especially since a friend who worked there had assured Andrew that he would be set up with a recruiter who would shuttle him through quickly. For the second position, Andrew interviewed for more than a month, and, *after* being rejected, he got two separate calls from recruiters saying: "Hi, your résumé just crossed my desk, and we have to get you in here ASAP." For all their technical wizardry, the human resources department hadn't set up a reliable database of prospects and interview histories.

One of the worst interviews I had was with a large car-rental company. The recruiter would ask a question and then interrupt me only five to ten seconds into my answer. He didn't want to hear what I had to say. About ten minutes into the interview he seemed exasperated and moved closer to the table, looked me in the eye, and said, "As a language major, you have nothing to offer my company." I earned a BA in German and felt like he was mocking my choice of study. I've since worked for Microsoft, Pitney Bowes, and CompuCom, but I'll never forget how I was treated by that recruiter. I've rented cars on dozens of business trips and I've gone out of my way never to rent from that particular company because of him.

—Brett, liberal arts, University of Utah

A Silicon Valley software company called to tell me I was on their "wait list," with three people ahead of me. That was a total turnoff. I don't want to know exactly how many people they think are better than me! Eventually they made an offer, but instead of the usual "I got the offer" thrill, I was annoyed that I wasn't their first choice. They made me feel like they'd settled for me since they couldn't get their first (or second, or third) choice. It also made me wonder what was wrong with the company—why were so many people rejecting offers?

—Katie, engineering/science, Stanford University

FIVE WAYS TO WIN THE GOSSIP GAME

Playing the gossip game is a little like playing with fire, but you really don't have a choice. Some employers think it wise to lie low to avoid incurring negative buzz. Then they face the problem of nobody knowing who they are. In college recruiting, no news about your organization is not good news. Every day, every season, every year your stock is rising or falling in the eyes of your target recruits. There is no middle ground. Since you have to play the gossip game, you may as well play to win.

Hear the buzz

No matter how well you think you're doing, work hard to stay current with what your recruits are thinking and saying about you on and off campus. The automaker whose intern pipeline was destroyed by five MIT students complaining about their summer work experiences might have contained the damage had the company heard about it (or cared to get honest feedback from their interns). Stay tuned in and discover real or perceived problems soon enough to gain a chance to improve internships and limit the negative gossip.

Stay plugged in to key information providers on campus. A

recruiter from Goldman Sachs calls school staff every couple of months to ask what students are saying about the firm. Goldman Sachs knows they need as many ears to the ground as possible. Microsoft representatives are also known for frequently asking for the latest recruiting buzz on campus, not just about Microsoft but also about Microsoft competitors. College career counselors, staff, and faculty actually tell those company representatives the truth because Microsoft recruiters have shown that they care enough to act on the feedback they receive. Microsoft's inquiries are more than lip service, whereas other organizations simply go through the motions of asking. Companies that don't act on the information they receive prove that they don't really care, so campus information brokers don't bother to give them the entire story.

Finally, go online. Some of your best recruits are posting very candid thoughts about recruiting on blogs or public message boards. What they put on the Web is for everyone to see, so make sure you know what is being said about your organization. Google Blogsearch, Google Alerts, and Technorati are a few online services that can help you automatically monitor new things written about your company.

Choose your messengers

Your role in the gossip game is to plant seeds. Allow others to spread the message so it grows. To maximize the size and influence of the resulting buzz, aim for those students whose opinions matter most on campus. Befriend student leaders, whether they are officers of clubs or perhaps just the most professionally put together. Whether they work for your organization or not, when student opinion leaders think highly of you, other students will likely think the same.

Students don't want to be sold by a Very Big Company. They want casual partnerships with individuals who understand them. If you have a single contact who's engaging and listens to the students—bonus points if it's a recent alum—you'll see impressive results in your recruiting.

Endorsements from professors, career counselors, alumni mentors, internship directors, and others also mean a lot to students. Feed these influencers information about the latest and greatest things your organization has to offer and make it easy for them to spread the word. For example, you might invite a small group to an informal dinner where you describe a new position that hasn't yet been publicly announced. Your influencers will feel privileged to learn about the new position and even more inclined to share the news when you ask them to.

Keep recruiters enthused

Your recruits won't want to work for your organization if your own employees don't seem excited about working for you. Make sure your recruiting team is enthusiastic when campus recruiting season starts. Host a dinner or party to remind your team why they like working for you in the first place. Some companies have been known to schedule promotion announcements right before campus recruiting starts and then strategically put the newly promoted people on the recruiting team. However you do it, get your people motivated at just the right time.

Keep summer interns enthused and motivated, too. When interns leave at the end of the summer, their next stop is campus, where they talk about their time with your organization as they settle into the new academic term. You want interns to walk out of your office as happy as can be so you get a good review. Take them out to dinner and celebrate the good work accomplished over the summer. Be generous with company T-shirts and other tchotchkes they can give to their friends.

Praise interns and entry-level employees in front of their friends. A Bain & Company representative really gushed over the hard work of a group of summer interns at a public information session and told the audience the interns had been extended full-time offers. One of the interns was so pumped by the praise that when he was asked to speak about his intern experience, he accepted the firm's full-time offer in public. The roar in the room seemed to last for days on campus.

Sweat the details with every recruit

You can't afford to ignore small transgressions like forgetting to make a call on the day you said you would. If you let one call slip, you're probably forgetting twenty. And for college students, a missed phone call *is* a big deal. Students don't have the experience to empathize with working professionals. They have no idea how many calls don't get made and deadlines don't get met in the real world. In their experience, when they are told they will have an exam on Tuesday, 99 percent of the time they have an exam on Tuesday. Students expect the professional world to be just like school. Show too many students you've been out of school too long by ignoring deadlines and other details and your organization will pay.

The mile-a-minute mouths of college students are the ultimate amplifiers, so everyone involved in your organization's recruiting needs to understand that in every little encounter with one potential candidate you are really being evaluated by five or ten students.

One technology firm learned that an intern really wanted to become a doctor instead of an engineer. Rather than ignore the intern, as might happen in many organizations, the manager introduced her to a couple of family friends who were medical doctors. He even continued to mentor her and give her challenging work. The intern continued to work hard throughout her internship, and when she returned to school in the fall, she told all of her friends interested in that industry that they should work for the company. What a win for the organization! The manager's common sense turned what could have been a dead-on-arrival internship and subsequent negative gossip on campus into some productive work and a good dose of free advertising for the company: *This company will care for your career, even if you decide to change paths later.*

When you have a problem, fix things fast

When customers in restaurants complain about an order being botched, their mood often turns from enraged to ecstatic if the staff simply handles the situation in a professional manner and offers an appetizer on the house.

Mistakes happen. When they do, apologize to your recruits and do your best to make it up to them. For example, if you learn that an intern or new hire is stuck on a fluff assignment, get her moved to a priority project. She will quickly forget about her initial problem and applaud you for taking prompt and direct action. And don't be afraid to openly address past recruiting problems in public on campus. If you are aware of negative gossip being spread about your organization from a previous recruiting season, tell the new recruits how you have addressed the issues.

If you don't want to discuss past problems, then go out of your way to show the new recruits that you have changed your ways. For example, if your recruiting process was disorganized the previous year and you didn't get back to people when you promised, announce your team's policy that you'll get back to people after interviews within 48 hours and that your entire process, from application submission to offers extended, is one month, or whatever your fixed time frame is. Setting expectations and meeting them builds trust with your recruits and repairs your image on campus.

❖ *Chapter Takeaway:* Your prospects are as talented at sharing stories and spreading opinions as they are at academics. To help keep the buzz in your favor, check in with information brokers on campus and online. Remember that in addition to the work, salary, perks, and culture you offer, students talk about how you execute details of the recruiting process, including seemingly small things like whether you return phone calls and stick to deadlines. If you do mess up, there's opportunity to gain goodwill by fixing things fast.

PART TWO

THE
RECRUITING MACHINE

Execution Separates the
Winners from the Losers

Understanding today's top recruits is an essential first step on the successful recruiting path. Armed with the knowledge you've acquired in Part One, you're now ready to consistently achieve stellar recruiting results. But to come by those results more easily each year, your college recruiting plan needs to become a robust, constantly humming machine. There are four key components to the recruiting machine: Identifying and attracting the students you want; selling those prospects on signing with you; managing their lives inside and outside your company once they're on the job; and leveraging former interns and current employees to get the feedback you need for improvements and to refill your talent pipeline each year.

Back in the eighties, you could simply attend a campus career fair, host an information session, post job descriptions, and magically have scores of students clamoring to work for your organization. As recently as a few years ago, you could still have an edge by advertising your open positions on Web sites like Monster and HotJobs. But those days are long over. And the good news for you? Most employers—your competitors—do not realize those days are over.

Most of your competitors still set up the same old booths in the sea of others at career fairs. They post flyers on bulletin boards around campus. Then they leave campus disappointed by how few students show up at their information sessions and apply for their jobs. But you can and will identify and attract the students you want to work for you. You beat the brush for your best prospects. You improve on the standard ways of getting students to pay attention. And while you're doing these things, you keep in mind the following mantras: *Contact is king. Sell your people first, your company second. Courtesy and class go a long way.*

Contact is king. In the war for talent, contact is king, and personal contact is more important on the college-recruiting front than on any other. Your target recruits have little to no work experience, and will take the leap to their first full-time job—which means committing more than 40 hours of their lives each week to your organization—only when they like the people in your organization. The only way they can come to like you is by getting to know you through genuine, repeated personal contact.

Microsoft recruiters are often more visible on campus than are university employees. Their top priority is to meet personally as many target recruits as possible. They're in the audience at sports events, fine arts performances, and academic competitions, taking the time to see a past intern in the play or to watch a potential recruit win an award. Microsoft's recruiters actually form real relationships with the students. That kind of contact will enable you to woo top talent, too.

Sell your people first, your company second. Recruiting is the nexus between sales and human resources. Your job is to sell an experience, a career, and a way of life to a potential recruit through your people. Recruits can best appreciate your organization by actually meeting and learning how this experience and way of life has benefited their potential colleagues. So sell your people first, your company second.

Well-known companies often forget to tell recruits about their people and don't offer recruits the chance to meet them. Instead, they talk up their companies, mentioning quarterly earnings and increases in market share. Even if you work for an organization lesser known than the Citigroups and Wal-Marts of the world, you can compete with the big boys for ambitious recruits. Introduce students to your talent and save the scoop on quarterly earnings for your board of directors. Your recruits want to know that you're passionate about your job, how you got there, and where you started.

Courtesy and class go a long way. College students note well which employers mind their manners and which don't. Keep your cool and show courtesy and class to *all* prospects, and you will distinguish yourself from the competition. And minding your p's and q's keeps you out of the rumor mill, too.

4

Identify and Attract

Beating the Brush for Your Best Prospects

Where are the best prospects? You know they're out there because top companies are getting them. The more important question is, Where are *your* best prospects? That's the real trick to playing the game alongside Microsoft, McKinsey, Google, and other recruiting behemoths: having a clear picture of your best prospects and knowing where to find them. This calls for equal parts research, networking, and creativity, and if you stick to your mantra, all your hard work will pay off in spectacular prospects that are just right for *you*.

CHOOSING COLLEGES

If the top ten recruiting companies get 50 percent of their recruits at, say, the University of Texas at Austin, the University of Virginia, the University of Pennsylvania, the University of California at Berkeley, and Northwestern, shouldn't you be recruiting there, too? Maybe, if you're in the same industry as the monster recruiters. And maybe not, if your best prospect is at the top of his class at a lesser-known or smaller school. You have to create a profile of your prospect, and to do that you need to know the profiles of the academic institutions that might be developing your prospect right now. While the big guys are shopping for recruits at the Bergdorfs or Neiman Marcuses of the world, you may find your one-of-a-kind prospect in a small boutique around the corner.

How many schools do you need on your list? While there is no magic number, focusing on as few campuses as possible is practical and strategic when you keep in mind the need to make personal contact as often as possible. You need to think hard about where you most want to get your new employees so you'll know where to spend most of your time, money, and effort.

Unfortunately, many recruiters get stuck at this juncture because senior management has decreed that the organization will not fail to recruit the best students at the best schools—and, predictably, by "best schools" they mean not only the usual suspects (MIT, University of Pennsylvania, etc.) but also their own alma maters. But an investment banking analyst in Cleveland, for example, is not usually successful when his managing director sends him to recruit at the Ivy League's Columbia University simply because that's where the managing director went to school. Students are at Columbia because it's in Manhattan, and if they were interested in finance, why would they want to move to Cleveland when most of the best finance firms are just a subway ride from where they are now? This employer might have more success recruiting at schools like Northwestern, Michigan, or Carnegie Mellon because students who chose to study in the Midwest are more likely to give Cleveland a chance.

Recruiting at the boss's old stomping grounds is especially tough if you don't have any alumni in the junior ranks of your organization. If you recruit for a Texas energy company, having executives who graduated from Nebraska and Iowa twenty years earlier will be little help navigating those campuses now. Younger alum employees who can relate to a recruit's experience with a current professor or opinions about a recent campus event are more valuable assets.

Choose two categories of schools for your recruiting efforts. Category 1 contains your core schools. Category 2 contains your reach schools (the same as when you were applying to college yourself). The majority of your recruits should come from your core schools and a smaller percentage from the reach schools.

Companies often say they want to recruit only at "elite" schools, because they consider themselves elite. Sure, having some new hires from top schools adds cachet to your organization, but if your company doesn't have the resources to recruit well at those schools, then you should concentrate on getting the best students elsewhere.

Here are three questions to get you started in choosing your core and reach schools:

1. **Does the college produce students who share the same mind-set or core values as your organization?**

   Values are hard to change in people, even young people. A sample list of qualities you might want to consider—in your own order of priority for your unique organization—are work ethic, motivation, inclination to work with others, practical versus theoretical orientation, fun, and entrepreneurialism. For example, many employers choose to recruit from top-ranked engineering schools because those institutions pride themselves on instilling students with the will to do whatever it takes and work as long as necessary to get a job done. Other colleges produce students with different, but equally desirable, core values.

2. **Does the college produce students who have the skill sets that you want?**

   Most employers naturally think about skill sets. Some want computer programming in particular languages, foreign language proficiency, or experience leading a team project to completion. Others look for the ability to learn quickly and adapt, and many employers actually prefer a liberal arts background to a very focused technical one because the students are more used to approaching problems in all sorts of contexts. It's fine to look for specific skills, but it's dangerous to place more importance on skills than on values. A recruit who needs some training but is the right values fit for your organization is better than one who can't stand your organization but is the Tiger Woods of whatever it is you do.

3. **Where do I have the resources and support to recruit well?**

This question requires a two-part answer. The first is which schools will actually excite your recruiters. Alumni representation can sometimes energize entire organizations, so factor the enthusiasm your people have for specific schools into your available resources. Second, do you have the time, talent, and money to be successful at recruiting students from these schools? Time and money are self-explanatory, and talent, in this case, means your current reputation on campus (if any) and the alumni support you can expect from people in your organization. If you have alumni, use them! Get them excited about going back to their alma maters. And tap their knowledge of where to find the best students on campus.

If you're starting a college recruiting program from scratch, it's more important to spend your initial time researching which schools to approach rather than planning tactical moves. Plenty of retail companies, for example, tried to recruit at Stanford and left after a few years—and a lot of expense. The students simply weren't a good fit for their organizations.

If you have some data from past recruiting efforts, use it. Pay special attention to any distinct patterns in how performance in your organization has correlated with which colleges people attended.

ASSESSING CULTURE AND FIT

Angela Heyroth, College/MBA Recruiting Manager
Echostar Communications Corporation,
Englewood, Colorado

The school selection process for us is mostly about culture fit and relationships. When we evaluate schools, we're not looking for stats like average GPA or the ranking of this major versus that major. We look at the other companies recruiting on campus. If we see schools where every other company is a bank or financial firm, that's great for us because we can tell the students, "We're not a bank," and the kids who aren't interested in banking are naturally attracted. We stopped recruiting at another school where there were so many other media and communication technology companies that we were just one in a crowd.

We also look for student mobility. Even though we have 200 locations and we're a global company, most of our positions are in Colorado. So for college students, we look at where they went to high school, and for graduate students, where they went to college. Because if we recruited at a school outside Colorado where almost every student came from that state, they're probably not going to want to move to work for us. I don't care if our recruits come from Colorado or Oklahoma or Kansas or California or wherever, but we need to see they are willing to move to where we are.

You can tell right away if there's a culture fit when you call the school's career center. Pay attention to the type of questions they ask. Some ask arbitrary questions like "How big are you? What are your locations?" That's a sign that they don't really care about who you are. But if they ask more specific questions like "What kind of people are you looking for?" and "Why are you interested in coming to our campus to recruit?" then we know to ask more specific questions about their students and we can begin to create a relationship.

We have a great relationship with Denver University, for example, because the career development manager there understands how we like to work. When we say, "We don't want to recruit normally. We don't want to post preselects. We don't want to recruit this way and that way, and we're going to break all the rules. Are you okay with that?" The right person for us says, "That's great." Then we're excited. But if the school is not flexible enough to deal with us, then the school is off our list.

If a school is regimented then their students are probably regimented, too. That's a fine quality for some but it's probably not going to work for our organization's particular culture.

Note whether or not you seem to be rejecting an unusually high number or giving offers to a disproportionate number of interviewees from one university in contrast to other schools. Call the school and chat with their career office about the culture and desires of the students. By spending your time focusing on *which* schools to target, you can ensure you have an audience of students who are the right fit for the culture of your organization. Then you can strategize how to close the deal.

EXTENDING YOUR REACH

To extend your reach beyond a short list of target schools, you can easily and cheaply advertise jobs online for which any college student can apply. First-round interviews by phone won't cost you more than a few dimes, and some students, if they're hungry enough for the openings you have, will cover their own cost of traveling to your site for a final screening. But cases like that are rare. Better channels for extending your reach and accessing a bunch of students who possess the values and skills you need might not be universities at all. Here are three types of organizations through which you can access great potential recruits with less competition than you face on campus from other employers.

Scholarship programs

Plenty of foundations and organizations offer scholarships to students before and during college based on criteria such as academic excellence, leadership, community involvement, and athletic achievement. In effect, they have already found some of the most talented and motivated students, and the best organizations maintain ties with award winners by hosting reunions and keeping an active e-mail list. Find a scholarship program that is in touch with its past award recipients and you may have another direct, no-cost route to outstanding prospects.

Patti Ross, vice president of the Coca-Cola Scholars Foundation, said her team is eager to pass on great professional opportunities to its past award winners.

"We're so invested in our scholarship winners, we try to do whatever we can to help them succeed in college and throughout their careers," Patti said. "Some job opportunities are relevant to all of our Scholars. Other job postings are targeted, so we search our database for specific age ranges or college majors. And since we've started getting more and more opportunities recently, we're working on a job board for our Web site that Scholars can check periodically."

The following is an actual e-mail that Patti sent to Coca-Cola Scholars on behalf of a corporate partner that led to a quality new hire:

To: Coca-Cola Scholars
From: Patti Ross, Vice President, Coca-Cola Scholars
   Foundation

As many of you know, one of our long-range plans is to provide Coca-Cola Scholars with great opportunities for networking and employment. In the not too distant future, our Web site will have the capability to post these announcements, but until that time we will continue to rely on blast e-mails.

This e-mail contains a message from a talent scout and a senior director, who was also a 1990 Coca-Cola Scholar, at [COMPANY NAME DISGUISED]. They will be attending a reception that Coca-Cola Scholars Foundation President Mark Davis is hosting at the Coca-Cola offices in Washington, DC, on June 15 (if you are in DC and have not received an invite, give us a call).

We feel so fortunate to be able to partner with [COMPANY NAME DISGUISED] on this initiative, as this is a relationship that may very well provide opportunities for some of our Scholars.

As always,
Patti

In addition to the Coca-Cola Scholars Program, you may find other potential partners, such as the Ron Brown Scholars Program or Hispanic Scholarship Fund, through the National Scholarship Providers Association (www.scholarshipproviders.org). However, famous national scholarship programs aren't the only options. Smaller regional or local programs can help, too. Many service organizations like Kiwanis, Lions, and Rotary offer scholarships. The Kiwanis Club of West Palm Beach, for example, has an annual holiday lunch for all their award recipients. Attending events such as these is a wonderful way to meet promising students. Such clubs will be especially delighted if you're offering local positions, as one of their big goals is to cultivate contributing members in their local communities. And, obviously, if your organization has its own scholarship program, it should give you a huge leg up with some recruits.

My best recruiting experience was in Boston at one of the biggest career fairs I attended. I was talking to Toyota, who immediately pulled out all my info from when I won a Toyota scholarship in high school and talked to me like I was family. At first I thought it was weird but they seemed to appreciate everything about me and listened like there was no one else around. It made me want to work for the company even more.

—Kerrie, Stanford University

National student organizations

Most student groups on campus are actually chapters of large national or international organizations. Some, such as the National Society of Black Engineers or the Society of Hispanic Professional Engineers, were created to focus on professional development. They are especially prepared to work with employers, not only by putting you in touch with students via e-mail, but also by holding career fairs at their large conferences.

But don't limit yourself to these strictly professional-based organizations. Fraternities, sororities, service organizations, honor societies, and other special-interest groups can be great resources. The Model United Nations, for example, is an ideal place for employers—from the State Department to Teach For America—to access a wealth of students who can speak well, think on their feet, and navigate a bureaucracy.

By reaching students through national organizations, you're likely to find leaders *and* add diversity to your talent pool because the students are from colleges all over the country.

One such organization that does the filtering for you is Impact, a nonprofit student-run organization founded by Kunal Gupta, a student at the University of Waterloo in Ontario, Canada. Dedicated to promoting entrepreneurship in Canada, Impact sponsors Impact Apprentice, a program modeled on the popular television show *The Apprentice*. For its initial competition, Impact received over 300 applications and narrowed the applicants to 32 top business students. Representatives from Research In Motion, which makes the popular BlackBerry handheld devices, served as judges for the first event and joined the winning team for dinner. Executives from IBM did the same at the second event, and TELUS Communications treated winners of the third challenge to a hockey game. In all cases, the employers offered guaranteed job interviews to the competition winners as well. Another event, an elevator pitch competition sponsored by the angel investment fund Infusion Angels, resulted in the winner receiving an all-expenses-paid trip to New York to receive business mentorship from the executive team of Infusion Angels.

College alumni associations

Most universities have regional alumni clubs that sustain communities of alumni who support each other and the school. Many clubs keep job boards or publish newsletters in which employers can advertise open positions to alumni or current students from that college. Many times you don't even need to be an alum to post the position. Some alumni clubs are more helpful in reaching people who have already graduated, but others actually go out of their way to help current students from their regions find summer internships or full-time jobs.

YOU DON'T HAVE to partner with all of these groups to extend your recruiting beyond your target schools, but you can surely enjoy some low-hanging fruit by cooperating with a few that make the most sense for your organization's needs. By no means is this an exhaustive list of places to reach for recruits. You should always be on the lookout for others, because you never know where you'll find great young talent.

WHEN IN ROME

Now that you've targeted your schools, you need to know those schools like the back of your hand. Recruiters from Microsoft and McKinsey can talk about the curriculum of a particular school as though they have been through it themselves. These recruiters may even seem to be more in tune with what's happening on campus than some students themselves. You, too, can reach that level of familiarity with a campus and its students. Essentially, there are four ways to be fluent on campus.

Pretend you're applying

When you're recruiting at a college you didn't attend, do the "prospective student" thing: Browse the school's Web site, read every piece of propaganda from the admissions and information offices, and definitely take a formal campus tour. A tour is an hour well spent, not only because you learn all about the geography and history of the campus, but also because the tour guides are usually some of the school's most articulate, interesting, and motivated students—just the kind of people you're there to recruit!

Be an honorary grad

Pick up the lingo and all the common acronyms, check the activities calendar for big events, and memorize the key majors, popular classes, and favorite professors. Once you attain a graduate-level education about the college, students will think "You're one of us" when they meet you.

Watch the campus clock

Every campus runs on its own schedule. Some schools have their students up and in the classroom as early as 7 or 8 A.M. At other colleges, many students don't have their first class until 10 A.M. or later.

Before you schedule any event, check with students or university staff to confirm you've picked a good time. For example, all the varsity athletic teams and performing arts groups at many schools hold their practices from 4 to 7 P.M. daily; employers who want to recruit those students should know that 6 P.M. is a terrible time for information sessions. Evenings in the middle of the term won't attract recruits either. Not only have the students' workloads increased from the first of the term, but several of the largest courses administer exams then, too.

Just as important as learning the schedule of students is watching out for events of other employers. One young but prestigious bank trying to start a talent pipeline at a new campus seemed to have done everything right to attract students to its first information session of the year, creating exciting work opportunities for new recruits and spreading the word about their information session through students and university staff. One small oversight, though, destroyed the potential value of their event: They mistakenly scheduled their information session at a time when the big, established recruiting competitor was in town. The result: Only seven students showed up for their session. Shame on the campus-wise recruiting team for not knowing better.

Know the superconnectors

When an employer initiates contact with a school, a recruiter from the organization often begins by requesting meetings with a department head, thinking that faculty members who head large departments will have access to lots of students. While a department head *is* exactly the person to talk to if you are creating a formal research alliance between your organization and the university, he or she is rarely a great source of student contacts.

The real recruiting superconnectors actually know hundreds of students by face and first name and can't walk to the restroom or cafeteria without exchanging greetings and briefings with a dozen students and other college employees along the way. Sometimes these superconnectors are professors, but more often they are career counselors, academic advisors, and internship program staff. Athletic coaches, residence life staff, and department administrators—not the faculty chairs—are also good bets.

Ask students and staff directly who can help you with your campus recruiting efforts and keep track of the names that come up more than once. Ask for introductions and treat the superconnectors well. Develop a few strong relationships with the best superconnectors—they'll be invaluable in finding which students are really special and which ones aren't.

EVERY EMPLOYER HAS to piece together its own dossier on how each of its target schools operates and, from that, decide how to best recruit on campus. Schools don't compile this information in a booklet and make it available to recruiters. It's up to you to spend time talking to people and getting the lay of the land.

The Top Nine Campus Recruiting Spots

> The biggest mistake that employers make is relying only on traditional recruiting channels like career fairs and job postings to attract our students. General Motors has been extremely successful here because they are engaged in nonrecruiting activities as much or more than standard recruiting activities. It seems like their recruiter is everywhere. And when it's time to fill jobs, it really pays off.
>
> —Ernest Walker, assistant director for career services, Georgia Tech University

When you're actually on campus, you do not want to be perceived as a walking advertisement for your company that's all interruption and annoyance. For best recruiting results, locate places and organizations on campus where students will actively engage with you and naturally consider your message. The top nine recruiting spots, not all of which are traditional recruiting venues, include the following:

Career offices

The school career office is the hub of campus recruiting and a good first stop. But it can be so much more than the location of campus interviews and the office responsible for managing your job postings. Most career centers run events year-round to help students learn job-hunting skills like writing résumés and cover letters, interviewing, and networking. Volunteer to teach these programs. Career counselors love to get employers involved because it lends more credibility to the events and it lightens their own workload. Students are desperate to get advice from real employers, and the interaction with employers often becomes something of a personalized information session. Many students accept jobs from employers they meet at these events.

At the University of Houston, the career office in the College of Business has an advisory board comprised of several companies. Janna O'Neill, formerly the employer relations manager there, said, "Dynegy [an energy company] was particularly interested in recruiting honors students, so their membership on the board helped them gain access to the students they wanted."

Co-op and internship programs

Co-op and internship programs are great ways to meet students, especially if you are new to campus. A co-op program allows students to attend school and work for companies in alternate semesters. Usually, co-op assignments are six months long, and often students in formal university co-op programs return to the same companies throughout their college years and beyond. At Northeastern University, for example, approximately 6,000 students each year work at more than 1,500 co-op sites or companies in Boston and across the United States. Nearly 40 percent of Northeastern graduates are offered permanent employment through one of Northeastern's co-op employers. Students in this program get to know their co-op advisors early on in their undergraduate years and the relationships formed are invaluable for future recruiting efforts within the companies.

Hiring students for three- to six-month work intervals is a significantly lower risk for your organization than hiring full-time employees right away. And college staff who run co-op and internship programs can become an extension of your recruiting team.

Intern program staff know their students really well because their job is to place each individual student in a meaningful work experience. Furthermore, staff performance evaluations are usually tied to how many students they successfully place. As long as you have a good experience to offer their students, they will bend over backward to help you. When you describe what you're looking for in new recruits, they should immediately be able to think of the handful of students who would best fit your organization. That alone saves you some of the time and hassle usually associated with recruiting at career fairs.

School internship programs also host professional development events such as interview training nights, résumé critique sessions, and meals combined with networking sessions. The school coordinates and pays for these events, and the employers just have to show up. An engineering manager from General Electric Aviation volunteers at MIT UPOP events every year. She gets to meet a large number of students, and the program office makes a special effort to find qualified students for her company because they appreciate the time she spends helping to teach the development sessions.

Externships and job shadow programs

A short, unpaid mini-internship that ranges from a few hours (job shadowing) to up to a month (the longest externships) are often

ideal opportunities to connect with students. There's much less selling involved than for an internship program because students are
mostly carefree about committing to an assignment of a month or
less. You don't pay the students, so there are no budget constraints.
The only thing required of you is that you find quality assignments
for the recruits to take and interesting people for them to work with.
While you will have a lower percentage of externs than interns return to work for you, it's a cheap and easy way to develop stronger
relationships with students. Ultimately, those relationships grow
your presence on campus, especially when your externs tell friends
about the positive experiences you provided.

A Wharton alumnus who runs a small firm in New York allowed Wharton students to apply to spend a day in his office learning about his
job. In addition to teaching me a lot about his firm and industry, he
treated me to a great lunch. We kept in touch via e-mail and met
again for coffee when he came to campus. That's when I received an
offer to work at his firm over the summer. I think his method of recruiting was effective because it cost him very little time and expense.
Wharton Career Services screened applications for the day at the office and made the final determination, so the alum was assured the
most promising potential interns.

—Robin, business/economics, University of Pennsylvania

Different offices at different universities administer externship
and job shadow programs, and sometimes there are multiple externship programs running on a single campus. Ask about posting in the
career office, but talk to superconnectors about other great ways to
advertise your externships.

Classrooms and laboratories

Injecting your recruiting into students' academic coursework is a big coup. Although this can require intensive legwork and some professors just won't allow it, it can deliver great results if you can pull it off. To get in the classroom you might give a guest lecture in a class, judge an in-class competition or project, or have your company mentioned in the homework sets or tests. The tricky part is meeting the professor who will let you do this. Ask students directly which instructors are especially good at relating coursework to real situations in industry, and offer something valuable. Treat this as a partnership, not just a marketing opportunity. At the University of Southern Maine, the School of Business has created a program in which students can work in teams to tackle real problems that local companies are experiencing. Ann, an accounting major who has worked with companies as part of two recent classes, said, "The program is a win-win because students get real-world experience working with companies like L.L.Bean and TD Banknorth, and the companies get free consulting and access to students they might want to hire."

If your company is collaborating with faculty on a research project, it should be even easier to get your foot in the door of a lab. Ask the professor to put you in contact with undergraduate or graduate students on her research team. Researchers from your organization may think of the possibility for recruiting while working on a joint project, so your recruiting team should politely remind the company

> I probably never would have considered working for Schlumberger if I hadn't worked with them on my research project. I didn't know much about them before that.
>
> —Logan, engineering, MIT

representatives on the project to relay useful information and to share stories about work at your organization. It pays off.

If your organization doesn't sponsor academic research, you can still get to potential recruits with a little research of your own. Browse professor's research profiles on the Web to see which ones are doing projects that relate to your company's work, then ask the professor to connect you to the students participating in the project, or, if the students are listed online—and they often are—contact them directly. The students will be flattered that you sought them out.

Academic department headquarters

University staff responsible for the administration of specific departments are among the most underrated recruiting helpers because employers don't understand how much student contact these administrators have. They often know more students than faculty do. And while their primary job isn't to find internships and full-time positions for students, they have a vested interest in their departments' students finding good work opportunities because high placement rates make their departments look attractive.

Perhaps the most attractive thing about partnering with department administrators is access to their e-mail lists. Students are much more likely to read an e-mail message if it comes from an academic authority figure. For example, the job e-mail list for the department of electrical engineering and computer science at MIT is probably the most well-known and well-read e-mail list on campus, and the administrator who manages that list knows many undergraduate students personally.

Competitions

College students participate in many types of department, campuswide, national, and international competitions—in robotics, mechanical engineering design, art, speech, business plans, and solar

DIAMONDS IN THE ROUGH

Students at every college get filtered out of standard recruiting processes, even though they might be great fits for your organization, because of their GPAs or other parts of their résumé that don't meet your standard requirements. Of course, imposing thresholds like "Must have 3.0 GPA and at least one summer's work experience" is a good way to quickly whittle down a stack of résumés to a manageable reading load. But if you truly care less about how students are described on paper than what they can accomplish for you in the real working world, ask your campus superconnector friends for help spotting students you might have missed.

Daphne Nadal, an internship coordinator in the career center at the University of California at Irvine, said, "There are a lot of students out there, especially first-generation college students, who have been told by their parents just to focus on academics. Sometimes even by junior or senior year they don't have any work or internship or volunteering experience and aren't very involved on campus. But they have a lot of potential. They have great work ethics. You can see it in their GPAs and the class projects they've done. The best way to reach these students is to let career counselors know that you have opportunities for them. If you let the placement office know you have an opportunity for students like this, they will recommend you to the students."

If even the most desirable recruits are thrilled when employers take an interest in them, imagine how students who are just under the radar feel when employees show interest. Students are hungry for opportunities to work hard and prove themselves. Sometimes it's worthwhile to reach out and give them a chance.

car racing, to name a few. These are all great opportunities for you to see students showcase their skills and creativity and make contact with those who interest you. But focus on the contests that are best aligned with the profile of your target recruits. For example, in the mechanical engineering department at the University of Minnesota, sophomores participate in a robot-design competition as part of their curriculum. At the university's Roboshow, each student has the opportunity to showcase robots and present strategies and methods to any guests. This event is open to the public and is extremely popular. High school students, parents, and—yes—employers are invited and encouraged to visit the 175 students at their booths in the competition. Employers are invited to judge the competition as well, allowing you to see bright technical minds in action and proactively approach the most promising students.

Once you know which competitions are best for you, you may even want to sponsor one of these events. You get more exposure as a sponsor than as a spectator, and you establish working relationships with the student leaders. But don't make the mistake of thinking that you can just pay students to set everything up. Many employers do that and then just show up at the event. This is absolutely the wrong way to think about event sponsorship because your event won't be the best it can be and you won't be taking the opportunity to get to know student leaders who could later work for you or help you recruit other talented students.

Gemini Consulting had an office two blocks from Harvard but had not recruited there in years. Bain, McKinsey, and the Boston Consulting Group—names that were sure to draw a crowd—already sponsored the largest business plan competition on campus. By becoming a cosponsor, Gemini assured itself a built-in audience. It just had to convince students that it could provide a special professional opportunity. The plan worked. Gemini attracted many applications, made several offers, and eventually hired the lead student organizer of the competition.

Student groups

There are countless student groups with e-mail lists and events you may want to tap into, but take care to choose groups that match the profile of your ideal recruit. Consulting companies, for example, have tight relationships with the consulting clubs on many campuses. Computer science clubs around the country receive so many job offers that they've set up specific e-mail lists for technology job posts. Matt Clemente, a junior at the University of Miami and president of the Biomedical Engineering Society, says that working with student groups is the best way to get students' attention at his school: "Our group will set everything up for visiting employers and usually will guarantee an audience." The trick to partnering with any student group is to ask the group if you can speak at one of their mandatory meetings for all members. The group won't give you a whole lot of time to present, but you will have a large guaranteed audience.

Also consider how different student groups promote an event. One company sent an e-mail offering to deliver a workshop on how to prepare for a career fair to the student business clubs at UCLA. One club, the Business Leadership Organization, asked the company to speak at their weekly meeting, and in exchange attendees would take a survey about their past recruiting experience. A description of the company's talk was sent to the group's leaders, and they advertised the event several times on their e-mail list and provided refreshments with the club's budget. Over fifty students attended—a golden opportunity for recruiting!

Clubs are always eager to have employers meet their students. Use your college staff contacts to refer you to the right students and you get even better results.

In addition to holding events, student groups sometimes publish booklets or compile electronic files of all their members' résumés. Whether the résumés are free or available at a nominal cost, get them. A software company recruiting on the MIT campus got zero résumés within two weeks of posting a job. Upon our recommendation, the recruiter bought the résumé book of a group in the computer science department and began directly contacting high-potential recruits. The book cost $100, but the employer quickly packed a two-day interview schedule.

The athletic department

Coaches, trainers, and athletic administrators have very strong relationships with students because of the extraordinary amount of time college athletes devote to their sports. And they also know students' leadership qualities, sense of responsibility, and ability to work in teams. Coaches and athletic directors often feel their athletes are at a disadvantage in the recruiting process, in part because recruiting events are usually held during practice hours and the campus career office is closed by the time practice is over. Therefore, these athletic administrators are usually eager to partner with employers. Propose dinner for a group of athletic teams, and set up a special information session or a professional development workshop. The athletic department may coordinate the entire event and give you the space to use at no charge.

Residential life

Student living groups—residence halls, eating clubs, fraternities, and sororities—are where everything that's *not* academic happens. Intramural sports, group dinners, parties, and, if you play your cards right, recruiting. Students will be more comfortable talking with you where they live than at the career fair for the same reason you prefer Starbucks to your cubicle for meeting a new contact. And the supervising staff—hall directors, graduate assistants, even student resident assistants—can be very helpful in identifying top talent because they know who students really are, not just the show they may be able to put on in a job interview.

Bain & Company went to residence halls and sororities to deliver workshops about case interviews that consulting and finance firms frequently use in recruiting. Attendance was high, not only because of Bain's great reputation, but because all a student had to do to attend was walk down the hall. Bain also sweetened the deal with a late-night snack.

When you set up an event in a living group, arrange to take a staff member like the residence advisor to dinner earlier in the evening. They'll enjoy the free meal as much as a student would because they are generally way underpaid. And if you explain what you're looking for, they can prep you for meeting the most promising students.

EVENTS STUDENTS LOVE

Typical information sessions just don't cut it anymore. Students don't attend. They feel they can get all the information you might present on the Internet, so why should they come to an information session and listen to what they already know. They're really looking for something different, something unique, something educational, something more than what they can get from your Web site.

—Michelle Foley, career services recruiting coordinator,
University of California at Irvine

When competition for recruits is fierce, many companies will throw events that make it seem like they are entertaining clients rather than recruiting college students. We've heard of companies sponsoring invitation-only golf tournaments, throwing tailgate parties before big football games, or hosting dinner and a cocktail reception for their most desirable recruits. If you can afford it, that's great. Some companies enjoy buying the biggest booth or throwing the biggest bash as a matter of pride. But if you can get the same results with less money and more creativity, all the better.

The right superconnectors get you access to the right students, but you also need the right events to attract those students and have them remember who you are. You are better off sponsoring four events with different campus groups and having 30 interested students show up each time (120 total) than placing ads in the newspaper for one big meeting of your own where 20 students show up. As for the order of events that you sponsor, start off slow to earn trust. Your first event can't be an open house or even "A Day in the Life of . . ." You may not have the reputation to draw a lot of students. Start with events that students will need to go to at some point anyway—events they are not just curious about but are desperate to attend, like résumé critiques and mock interviews. There you'll build credibility and acquire student allies to help you move on to bigger and better events.

Résumé critiques

Students value constructive criticism of their résumés from employers, but a résumé critique session actually doubles as a kind of interview for you. If you can, set up your own résumé event where you bring several people from your organization. If you are one of many employers at an event put on by a career center, make the most of the opportunity to meet students by volunteering to give additional help to students who want it at the end of the session. If all the employers meet with three students in the evening, and you get the chance to spend time with one more, you will have gotten 33 percent more value and expended the same overhead of time to travel to and from campus. This same advice goes for mock interview sessions, too.

Mock interviews

Practice interviews with industry professionals give students confidence for future "real" interviews, but mock interviews are perhaps even more strategic for you. Mock interviews are an opportunity for you to see students in their most natural state, not when they are nervous, as is often the case in a real interview.

Students are excited to attend mock interviews, especially if your organization is in an industry that has a reputation for using nontraditional interview methods. Management consulting companies use case interviews, for example, which offer a simulated business situation and ask the student to provide an analysis. A sample situation might be related to declining revenues: "My shoe business has been doing well for the last ten years, but recently our revenues are down. What can we do?" Case interviews call for good analytical skills and the ability to handle pressure. Management consulting firms that offer mock-interview sessions get to meet the best of the best before their competitors. They don't offer these sessions only to graduating seniors, either; they invite students from all grade levels and often lure underclass students who may have no idea what consulting is but who want to start learning interview skills early or in preparation for competitive internships. Many consulting companies invite one of their current employees—who must have done well during his or her interview—to undergo a "live" case interview in front of the audience. This adds to the thrill of seeing behind the curtain of how it's *really* done.

> I went to an interview workshop sponsored by Bain [& Company]. I learned so much about interviewing and met such nice and impressive people from Bain. I am definitely more interested in pursuing consulting now where it wasn't even on my radar before.
>
> —Lauren, sophomore, Duke University

How-to-Work-a-Career-Fair seminars

Students crave information from real employers about how to make the most of career fairs. They are grateful if you tell them what to say when they talk to a potential employer, what to wear (and what not to wear) to the career fair, how they can end a conversation with an employer, and how they should follow-up with the people they meet. Helping students and getting to know them in this way makes them remember and trust you when the real recruiting process starts.

A-Day-in-the-Life workshops

What do you actually do all day? Students want to learn about your work, but they don't want to feel like they are being evaluated when you tell them what you do in a formal "information session." An informal workshop, on the other hand, is a big draw for students, especially if your industry is one about which they are curious. If the event is held at the right time and with the right group, students will definitely attend.

UBS sponsors a two-hour class called Investment Banking 101, in which they explain the basics of the industry and answer all the questions students are too intimidated to ask one-on-one or in a more formal setting. Whether your business is financial services or automotive or something in between, a day-in-the-life workshop is one way to sell your industry—and what you do all day—as cool.

OPEN HOUSE AT YOUR OFFICE

Gemini Consulting didn't have a strong reputation on some campuses, but bringing students in to see their swanky *Architectural Digest*–style offices dramatically improved Gemini's on-campus buzz factor. Whether or not your office is a masterpiece of modern design, if your company is anywhere near a target school, set up a field trip for students to visit. Use a campus superconnector to round up students and schedule an open house on a Friday. The students who attend are yours to impress for at least 90 minutes, so pull out all the stops. Get them to meet as many people as possible, encourage them to ask questions, have them flip through your documents and sit in your chairs, and, of course, turn your back so they can raid the snacks in the break room.

❖ *Chapter Takeaway:* When selecting colleges to visit, focus on "fewer is better." The more time you invest learning about a particular school and its students, the more precisely you can reach great prospects through academic departments, cocurricular programs, and student clubs that suit you best. Build relationships with college staffers who have lots of contact with students, and you'll always be one phone call away from timely information or a recommendation for a recruit.

5

Improving Your Recruiting Staples

Career Fairs, Info Sessions, and Job Postings

A mom-and-pop shop needing only one talented new graduate can probably pull off a successful recruiting campaign using just the guerrilla tactics discussed in the last chapter. But as soon as you have the need to reach larger audiences and bring in more young talent, you'll probably want to also use standard plays like attending career fairs, holding information sessions, and posting on major job boards. Though we call them staples or standards, they can have big risks and big rewards. Just go through the motions and they can do more harm than good. Follow the guidelines in this chapter and you can gain an advantage over competing employers who take these things for granted.

CAREER FAIRS

Career fairs don't sound very flashy or cutting-edge, but the more students you're trying to hire on a campus, the more necessary it becomes to do career fairs. If your organization is going to spend $1,000 or more on a booth and give up a day or two of several people's time to attend each fair, you may as well do them right. So be sure to keep in mind the following dos and don'ts to increase your return on investment.

Don't go if you're not hiring

If you are at a career fair, students expect that you are hiring for that recruiting cycle. You may not hire anyone that you meet at the fair, but you should go to a career fair with real positions in hand. You'd be surprised how many companies at career fairs are not hiring. If students find out that you are using the career fair to window-shop the talent, you may do more harm to your reputation than good.

> I was at a job fair, walking around and talking to employers. I went to the table of a pharmaceutical company, and after a brief conversation I asked what type of positions they were hiring for and they said, "We aren't hiring right now." Well, what's the point of getting me to talk to you for ten minutes at a job fair if you're not hiring? It's called a "job fair," not pointless conversation fair!
>
> —Megan, liberal arts, Connecticut College

Do your homework

Before you pay the registration fee, ask the career fair organizers for past attendance figures, a breakdown of majors and education levels of students, and their plan for attracting students to the upcoming fair. Run that information by your other staff and student contacts on campus to see if it's legit. Due diligence is the only way you can avoid becoming one of the many employers who have attended career fairs that had more companies than students.

Obsess over location

It matters more in large career fairs to situate your booth near heavy foot traffic than it does in retail and fast food to locate at the corner of a major intersection. Find out in advance exactly how the booth placement works. If, for example, attending employers are to be placed in alphabetical order, and your firm's name begins with a Z, you may want to become a higher-level sponsor of the career fair to swap your back-corner booth for a sweet spot by the entrance. Or you could suggest that placement be done in reverse alphabetical order every other year to be fair to every company attending. Lobby the organizers to provide multiple entrances, perhaps requiring students to enter specific doors as designated by their last names. Be prepared to get creative with the career fair organizers to set yourself up for success.

Do your own advertising

No matter how much advertising the career fair organizers plan, you should still do some of your own. The fair's advertising might list the name of every employer, but unless you're the lead sponsor, your name probably won't be noticed. Have your superconnectors forward an e-mail advertisement to students, letting them know you will be at the fair and that you want them to visit your booth. Many schools offer services that post flyers for you in dorms and other campus locations.

Make your booth double as a traffic sign

Your greatest challenge at well-attended career fairs is to get the students you want to approach your booth and to turn away less desirable students politely and quickly. To do this, your booth should display, in the largest and easiest-to-read lettering you can manage, not just the name of your organization, but also the exact divisions that are hiring, what your company actually does, and what attributes you want hires to have, so anyone can glance at it and know whether they should stay or walk away. Some employers tell us they purposely don't reveal any information other than their company names in hopes that students will be curious enough to approach and ask. Bad idea. If you don't have a universally recognizable name like Microsoft, Amazon.com, or Bank of America, you will miss out on students. They'll see your company name, have no clue what you do, and just keep on walking—unless you have the coolest toys to give away (see next section). But why waste money and time attracting students who want toys but don't want to join your organization?

Give recruits something to talk about

Think about displaying a cool product your company makes, or an eye-catching demo, or even videos of your awesome office spaces in different cities. Dramatic visuals or interactive displays are far more effective at creating word-of-mouth buzz than having your logo printed on a pen. Even if you don't have things to show, make sure that what you tell students about your organization emphasizes proven career fast tracks, perks and special treatment, and all-stars they could work with when they join your company. One equipment manufacturer put a sign next to the company name advertising work opportunities in Europe. That was enough to draw lots of students to find out more.

Get your whole team on the same page

Every representative from your company needs to be able to sell your industry, your company, and your new-hire program. When employers just grab any warm body from the office for the career fair, students notice and it hurts your chances of attracting the best.

Even if you think everyone on your team should know what to say, prepare a cheat sheet with details about the training program, a list of recent hires and alumni from that school, and some good examples of new-hire projects. It's a waste of your organization's time and talent if you end up with representatives passing students off to the one rep who actually knows her stuff.

It's rare to meet employers who seem like they really enjoy talking to me at career fairs. But it's even worse when they act like they don't know anything about the job I want to apply for.

—Jessica, engineering, North Carolina State University

Be nice to everyone

Each and every student who approaches your booth is a potential employee or a friend of one—so treat everyone well. Too often employers rudely dismiss students who don't exactly fit the profile of their target recruit. College students gossip like crazy, and the last thing you want to do is to make a negative impression on any one of them.

I went to the booth of a telecom company late in the day of a career fair. I approached the guy standing behind the table who was clearly counting the minutes until the fair was over, and he tried to ignore me. I asked him about his company and potential internships, but he just grabbed my résumé and said that they weren't looking for summer interns yet. Why send someone to a career fair if they aren't going to portray your company in a positive way?

—Julie, science/engineering, MIT

If you want to get rid of people, at least throw 'em a bone

Some employers at fall career fairs want to talk only to seniors for full-time recruiting, and they plan to return in the spring to recruit

A recruiter from a Silicon Valley Internet company really turned me off, even though I was very interested in the company. At the job fair booth, I was trying to ask him for some information about the opportunities at the company, and all he cared about was whether or not I had taken a particular class at Stanford. The recruiter would not answer any of my questions after I told him I hadn't taken the course, saying that he would not hire anyone who has not taken this class at Stanford. I was insulted and never applied after that.

—David, engineering, Stanford University

summer interns. Underclass students approach their booth only to be curtly turned away with a "We're only looking for seniors right now." This is a huge mistake and missed opportunity, especially because the few underclass students who have their acts together enough to job-hunt in the fall are probably the kind of people you want in your organization. Have a flyer that details your intern program and future recruiting events. If you don't have those details set, at least post a sign that says, "Interns: We will be back for you in the spring," so potential interns will feel like you care about them and get the message that you're just focusing on full-time hires for now.

Show a student who is not in your target group how she might get into your target group. It's always better to tell a student what *can* be done rather than what cannot. Let's say you're recruiting for a special program that hires only graduate students but an undergraduate approaches you. State that you hire only graduate students for the program, describe the graduate studies you require, and point the student to a Web site where she can learn more. Let her know that while the program is not for her, she should apply for the jobs (described on a flyer) that are for undergraduates. Tell her you are returning on a specific date to recruit for those positions. If the student doesn't let up, politely say, "It's been a pleasure meeting you," hand her your business card, and invite her to contact you by e-mail if she has further questions.

Pack your Pemmican

Remember that catchy jingle for the beef jerky that's supposed to keep your hunger in check during tough, long days? "Pack your Pemmican, and you'll survive the day!" Career fairs can be grueling—some lasting upwards of six or eight hours. You have to be *on* the entire time because you never know when the perfect candidate is going to walk up to your booth. Plan ahead to endure the entire day and bring enough representatives so that you can take breaks and alternate shifts. When you're really running ragged, step out for ice cream with a handful of students. They will concentrate on the ice cream and not notice that you seem a bit tired.

Send a personalized e-mail to every student you meet

I am always surprised and thrilled when an employer calls me on the basis of a résumé that I barely remember submitting. It's great to make a strong personal connection early on in the process instead of just sending my information off into the black hole of the Internet and hoping for the best. It makes me feel good both about myself (they like me!) and about the company (they know what they're doing!).

—Casey, science/engineering, MIT

Yes, you can use some technical tricks to limit some of the labor here, but if you don't get the students' first names right, don't bother. Ideally, you'd even make a quick note of something unique you remember about each one. College students are impressed when they get a real, personalized e-mail from an employee at a company they admire. Nothing guarantees a better response than this simple step—and you can stack the odds of positive buzz in your favor.

INFORMATION SESSIONS

Most information sessions are pretty boring and don't really help you figure out if you want to work for the company. They usually just read stuff off a PowerPoint presentation that I could read myself on their Web site.

—John, economics, Emory University

The information session is where students expect to be sold on working for you. They want to learn something insightful about the industry you're in, what's so special about your organization, why your new-hire program would be good for their careers, and what their predecessors have done after working for your company. Here are the keys to executing an event that does all that and leaves your recruits excited about applying for your positions.

1. **Again . . . location, location, location**

    Reserve a room on campus that's easy to get to and has plenty of open space away from desks, chairs, and tables for the crowd you plan to attract. The last thing you want is to be cramped up in a tiny classroom with 100 people. If you're trying to portray the wealth of a Wall Street juggernaut, consider renting space off campus to lend some cachet to your event. Most finance and consulting firms opt for a nice hotel to separate themselves from typical employers who use free space on campus, but that's not always necessary. You should be able to get great space on campus by asking one of your staff contacts to recommend and even reserve a room for you. A university's internal student organizations often get higher priority and better selection in room reservations, so work through one of them if you can.

2. Time it right

Consider exams, athletic practices, games, and other popular campus events when you schedule your information session. If you run into unavoidable conflicts, offer your session at multiple times.

3. Recruit your attendance and have them RSVP

You have to recruit students to attend the event before you can recruit them to work for your company. Send e-mail invitations through your superconnectors on campus and remind every student and staff you know to remind their student friends. Request that students RSVP by a certain date to avoid attendance surprises. Many students won't RSVP and will show up anyway; however, if *nobody* RSVPs then you and your superconnectors will at least have a chance to decide whether to drum up more interest or call it off. Post tasteful signs at the event's location, and when you arrive, stand outside the room or even outside the building at the entrance or near a major walkway to announce the event's start to all passersby. You can bring in many students at the last minute.

Everyone is usually really fake at info session events. Most recruiters don't seem genuine.

—Sara, business/economics, University of California at Berkeley

4. Get the right speaker

You've done so much work to gather a captive audience that you can't afford to put out a lead speaker who's not ready for prime time. Your career fair speaker is the face of the company for students who are just becoming acquainted with you, so choose wisely. And remember the mantra, "Sell your people first, your company second."

Despite the fact that the firm of Capgemini was relatively unknown at MIT, there was always a buzz on campus after the firm's information session because their lead presenter, a star manager, sold himself so well without making the students think the talk was only about him. Every student left hoping to get to work with him or to be him! That's exactly what you want them to say about your speaker.

Some companies send just any senior officer, hoping that students will be impressed by a fancy title. Of course, a fancy title may seem cool at first, but if your VP of whatever is only an average show- and salesperson, the students will leave thinking, *I don't want to work at a company where they think someone like that is a star. They must not be very good.*

5. Talk up potential career paths and the most glamorous parts of the job

Tell plenty of real stories about real people who have had opportunities to advance in your company. Give students sound bites they can use to brag to their friends, such as, "In our investment banking division, Mike made managing director before age thirty." Also, injecting a description of what you do that their parents can understand will be much appreciated. For example, a management consulting firm might say, "We're kind of like doctors for businesses. We help other companies solve their problems."

6. Bring as many alumni as possible

Alumni are living case studies of the career paths students want to be reassured of over and over. Meeting alumni gives students a vision of how to go from college student to successful professional, with your organization helping them through the transition.

7. Be clear about the next steps

Be sure to tell new recruits the obvious: exactly how to apply and what the rest of the recruiting process entails. Spelling it out clearly increases the chances they'll actually do it.

8. Have everyone sign in

Use notepads, pens, and a bit of vigilance to get the names, years, majors, and especially the e-mail addresses of all the students in the room. You then have permission to follow up with students, even if they forget or choose not to apply. Ask them to note how they heard about your meeting so you can measure the effectiveness of your marketing channels. Use the sign-in list to send a personalized e-mail to every person who attended. This step is worth the time—especially since your competitors aren't doing it.

9. After your formal presentation, meet as many students as possible (contact is king)

Demonstrate sincere interest in the students and try to get to know them.

Raytheon allowed us to talk with current employees, answered every single question, and told the negative and the positive. The one-on-one with their leaders after the talk really helped me to get a feel of the culture of the company. I had a great conversation with someone in upper management who had started from the bottom. We talked about investing and other topics, which, although not related to the job, made me feel we got to know each other. He said he liked the initiative that I had shown in talking to him, so he gave me his business card and later on he made me an offer for my next internship.

—Brian, engineering, Northeastern University

McKinsey's information session was amazing. They had about 20 current employees there to answer questions, at least 75 percent of whom were alumni. They also didn't bore you with a presentation, but left a lot of time for students to interact with the employees personally. They also had coffee chats the next day, which provided the opportunity once again for personal interaction. I feel as if the company values me, even if I don't receive an offer. I also received an e-mail to acknowledge receipt of my résumé within 24 hours of [my] having submitted it. I really get a good impression of the people who work for McKinsey by their desire to treat all their recruits as potential assets to their firm. As of now, I don't even know if I have an interview with McKinsey, but I can tell you I would attend the interview gladly, and likely not turn down an offer, if I were to receive one.

—Stephanie, biology, MIT

FIVE COMMON ON-CAMPUS ADVERTISING MISTAKES

Whether you are trying to get students to attend an event or to check out your job postings, avoid these frequently made mistakes.

1. **Wasting time and money on advertising that doesn't reach your target audience**

   Newspapers and bulletin boards may seem like great places to advertise, but do you know which day most students actually read the campus newspaper? And if they do read it, do they even notice the ads from employers? Before you spend thousands of dollars, ask ten students if they remember a recent advertisement and whether or not it got any of them to attend an event or apply for a job.

   Before you put up posters, ask students if they look at the bulletin boards. Find out which walls attract more eyeballs than the others, and know when the boards are cleared. One employer put posters up on every board at an East Coast university before he left campus on a Friday afternoon. Too bad the boards are completely cleared every Sunday evening, before students fill the halls again.

   Even if you decide to stick with sending e-mails through your superconnectors, find out when students are most likely to read them. Organizations often have success sending e-mails to students on Sunday because students have more time for e-mail then than they do during the week and are more likely to be at their computers working on Sunday than Saturday.

2. **Leaving students confused about who you are and what you're hiring for**

   If you are not Nike, Coca-Cola, or McDonald's, you have to briefly but clearly and memorably say what your company does. Even if you do have a recognized brand like IBM, you want to specify which division is recruiting and what it does, especially if it's not your core business unit. Investment banks have problems recruiting for their technology departments because students don't think *technology* when they see the name of a bank.

Don't list the boring and confusing titles of jobs that accounting or Human Resources uses for internal purposes. Use job titles or descriptions that students can understand. Nobody knows or cares what Engineer I or Technology Specialist Level II means, but they do like to see Design Engineer or Marketing Analyst.

3. Not targeting a specific group of people

If you're seeking juniors to apply for summer internships, make your intent clear. Don't waste time trying to get your announcement on the class mailing list of a senior seminar. If freshmen or sophomores see an ambiguous recruiting advertisement, they assume they aren't welcome. The same goes with majors: If you don't specifically say, "All majors are invited," the only students to attend will be those who think what they study is aligned with your core business.

Many premed and prelaw students want to take time off before entering graduate school. McKinsey and other consulting firms have picked off some great talent by putting out ads that say, "Before you go to law school, come to McKinsey." And, of course, they have groups like the student law society and the political science department distribute the message.

4. Not calling students to action

You're not in the business of making Super Bowl commercials that just remind people that Doritos exist. You're advertising for a reason, so tell students exactly what you want them to do: Apply at this Web site. Come to this room at this time.

5. Not mentioning the good stuff

In Boston, Mike's Pastry is famous, and any event on campus that offers free dessert from Mike's Pastry is going to draw a crowd. If your CEO is attending or you're giving away a new car or an iPod, proclaim it in your ads!

JOB POSTINGS

Job postings: Students are desperate to read them but employers dread writing them. One recruiter from a large conglomerate said her postings are structured the way they are because, "It's just what the database will allow. We have been following this format for years because that's what Monster wants." If this is the mind-set in your organization, don't bother saying you're looking for people with creativity and flexibility, because whatever amount of those two attributes the students possess will be erased forever by that attitude. The database does not control you. You control the database.

Employers are often unclear about who should write the job posting. Should it be HR or the business unit hiring manager? When nobody owns this task, it never gets done well. Work with your team to create a solution. Maybe both HR and the business units contribute, but HR has the final say.

Another challenge to producing great job postings is not knowing yet during the recruiting season what the position actually entails. This is especially common for employers who hire interns. Perhaps hiring managers know that a project is coming up soon, but they won't know their exact needs until another piece of work is finished. Work around this by describing as much as possible the group's goals and the two or three directions that the project may go. Or, describe what kinds of work similar new hires have done in the past.

Bottom line: The job post has to be compelling. Students often get excited about a job after hearing about it through friends or meeting an employer at a career fair, but when they finally read the official job posting online, they are turned off.

If you can sell students on a job and your organization with a well-written post, you get a huge return on your investment, especially when it doesn't take much more time to write a great description than an average one.

YOU ARE NOT GOOGLE

A technology company was recently disappointed when very few students applied to its job posting. The hiring manager was upset because he said he wanted only the "best" students, and clearly the best students did not apply for his position. When it was suggested that he didn't do enough to attract and identify the students that he wanted, his reaction was, well, "Google places ads like we do and has tons of students show up at their information sessions and career fair booths."

Any company does itself an injustice by comparing its recruiting tactics to Google's. There is more to Google's current recruiting success than meets the eye. It is a very young company with lots of employees who still have friends on college campuses. Rounding up students for information sessions is no problem, and print advertisements only supplement the effort. Google is a household name, used every day by seemingly everyone on college campuses and throughout the world. Google also enjoys the fabled reputation of having made many twentysomethings into millionaires. Even if the opportunity for creating fortunes is much less now that Google has gone public, the young-millionaire mythology continues to make college students line up for any event Google sponsors on campus.

So while Google can just build it and they will come, you can get a better, more strategic start by getting more personal contact with your target recruits.

The format for most job postings today is job title, company description, position description, and qualifications. In most campus recruiting databases, the first thing students see is a long list of job posting summaries, maybe 25 listed one after another. In the same way that you screen candidates by scanning headers on résumés, students decide whether to click through to your job post based solely on what shows up in the company name, job title, and location fields.

Company name. Obviously, you can't change your company name but you can give more information about it. Indicate what division of the company is hiring, but go deeper if you can. You may want to indicate the specific group within a division that is hiring, especially if the group seems more attractive. If you own a start-up or a firm that isn't well known, your company no-name is actually going to hurt you, unless right after it you can say in one line what you do and why it matters. Students are always attracted to brand names, but they are even more attracted to companies that change the world. Agamatrix is a young company that makes noninvasive blood glucose monitors for diabetes patients. Very few students recognize the name Agamatrix, but they all recognize the need for these devices. When Agamatrix's postings include a line stating that they research, develop, and produce state-of-the-art glucose monitoring systems, they attract more applicants. Also, you may be a small unknown company, but you may have impressive clients.

Job title. Internal titles such as Engineer I or Technology Analyst II do not communicate what the job really is. Titles for new college hires may sound general because those jobs *are* general, but you should make an effort to list titles that indicate what the student would be doing on the job. If that's not possible, add what type of student you are seeking: "Students from any major to develop complex systems in X and manage projects." Or, "Mechanical engineering backgrounds (controls preferred) to design new system for onboard communications satellite." While not specific, titles such as Program Manager, Project Manager, and Project Consultant are generally appealing to students because they believe the ambiguity suggests they can handle any kind of program, product, or project. Remember: *Gotta keep my options open.*

When students click through to your complete job post, it does not guarantee they are going to read it all and apply, so start with your best elevator pitch. Write a three- to four-sentence abstract to state what your company does and why it matters, what the position entails and why it matters, and maybe one or two of your best examples of how the job advances a career. This *cannot* be generic—its sole goal is to excite the student enough to read on.

SAMPLE ELEVATOR PITCH

Apectra is a boutique health-care consulting firm with offices in San Francisco, New York, and Colorado. We're currently hiring top students for our two-year analyst program. On any given day, you might be traveling to a client site, consulting with hospital administrators, or helping to design a compensation system. Our analysts work closely with senior consultants and travel for client meetings and international training. After completing the two-year program, Apectra analysts have gone on to graduate school at places like Harvard Law School and UCSF Medical School, while many continue their careers at Apectra as senior consultants. To learn more, please see the full job description. Apectra is looking for students who have demonstrated excellence both in and out of the classroom. Application deadline: November 15.

Company description. Most company descriptions sound the same, especially for Fortune 500 companies: "We have great people. We have outstanding opportunities for advancement. And we strive to deliver value to our customers and shareholders. Blah, blah, blah." Explain what your company does and why it matters in a way those students' parents will also understand. "Delivering value to our clients" does not pass the parent test, which is especially important for companies that are in the business-to-business arena.

Program/job description. There are two parts to the program or job description. Some companies admit new hires into leadership or training programs, hence the designation "program"/job description. Describe how this job supports the company mission and why it is important. Perhaps the job is truly the heart and soul of what the company does, and without the new hire's support, things would not happen. Does your company expect graduates of this position or program to become its future leaders? The second part of the description explains the role and responsibilities for the new hire. Most employers do this part well. The key is to provide as many details about the position as possible.

If the new hire's duties are threefold, describe all three parts to the job. For example, if one of the roles is to build a database and then to input data, analyze it, and make recommendations, say so. Students want to know that they get to do analysis and share their opinions in addition to data entry. Even if analyzing and making recommendations comprises only 20 percent of the new hire's time, mention it. Students are willing to do the grunt work if they think they will somehow influence others.

Use the description to dispel stereotypes, too. Engineering new hires may spend a lot of time in the lab but not every waking moment. Make sure that you outline other duties to accurately reflect the position.

Highlight anything glamorous about the job: Travel to Asia. Work with senior leadership. Remember the *who*, *where*, and *why* in addition to *what* the student will be doing. If your people are your best asset, then tell the students a bit about the background of the person that they will be working for, or at the very least a typical profile, with an example.

One small company noticed an impressive spike in applications when brief biographies of the students' impressive supervisors were added to the post. Students get to work with senior people more often in start-ups than in hierarchical Fortune 500 companies. If greater access to highly respected professionals is something you offer, don't leave that unsaid.

Career path and support. No matter what the database asks for, add a field or category for career path and support (if you can't add a separate field, just separate the text within one of the current fields). Be direct about where your opportunity can take new hires. State how long you expect them to commit to the advertised role and what's planned for when that time is up. Do you help them get to grad school (e.g., with test prep or tuition reimbursement), to another position internally at the same location, or to a position at another location or business unit? All is contingent upon interest, performance, and skills, of course, but you should lay out the opportunities clearly.

Give examples of where their predecessors are now. Statistics are helpful here, especially if most of their predecessors went on to similar places, like graduate school or professional school. But you can also share simple stories about one or two of their predecessors whose success was clearly enhanced by your organization. Highlight cases in which new hires advanced very far within the company, but also brag about people who worked at your company and leveraged that experience to do something exciting and meaningful elsewhere, such as starting their own businesses.

Perks. In some cases it is appropriate to show that you continue to woo and dazzle recruits once they are on the inside. Bain & Company used to tell recruits that when they saved money on client engagements, they put it into a team account so that when a successful project was completed, the money could be used on nice trips, dinners, and so on. One team at Google went to a trapeze-jumping event after finishing a large project. The firm rewards performance and delivers a perk at the same time!

How your team spends discretionary money shows your recruits what you value as an organization. Some companies throw fun parties, while others sponsor internal research competitions.

Logistics/interview dates. Let students know the exact dates of when you plan to interview promising candidates. This gives them an idea of when they should expect to hear whether you'd invite them to continue the recruiting process.

Writing style. This is the last point and the most important. The writing style of a job post matters more than most companies realize. Students look for excitement, opportunity, and challenge. Unfortunately, nothing screams *Office Space* more than a poorly worded post riddled with corporate-speak. Write your job post and show it to your young employees. Ask them, "What would you change?" Use contractions. It's possible to sound unpretentious and collegial while still being serious about business.

See the sample job postings in the appendix for more ways to improve your own.

❖ *Chapter Takeaway:* Don't take for granted how you approach career fairs, information sessions, and job postings just because you've done them before and it seems like run-of-the-mill recruiting. You can dramatically increase the effectiveness of your on-campus appearances and advertising by adapting them to the inner workings of the campus and your understanding of the student mind-set. At each stage in your recruiting process, refer to Part One of this book to check how you can show more care for recruits' careers and find creative ways to provide some sizzle.

6

Making the Sale

The Interview and Offer Process

Many employers recruit like car dealers sell. They do a wonderful job attracting students, but the moment a student applies for the job, the employer stops wooing and starts grilling—the same way the friendly car salesman leaves you alone, face-to-face, with the financial specialist after the test-drive. Most employers think their job is to sell students on applying, and after that it's the student's job to sell the employer on hiring.

While interviews are absolutely an opportunity for candidates to further show their own worth, your prospects are also evaluating

---

I met my future boss for my interview in a Thai restaurant and we talked shop for hours. He asked what I thought the company should do with new ventures. He shared where he thought the company and industry were going. And by the end of the interview I didn't care what salary the company was offering; I had made such a deep professional connection with the interviewer that I would have worked for pennies.

—Brad, science/engineering, University of California at Santa Barbara

> I interviewed at a prominent law firm for a summer internship and felt very uncomfortable. The interview was formal and structured and the office itself was very quiet, almost as if people were afraid to talk. I didn't get a sense of camaraderie. After that I was sure I did not want to work there.
>
> —Jane, recent graduate, humanities, Stanford University

you throughout the interview and offer-making process. You have to sell your company continually at every stage of the game—when you conduct interviews, make offers, and celebrate acceptances.

Microsoft, McKinsey, and the best recruiting employers get more of the top recruits they want because they know to use the interview process as an important sales tool, and they carefully manage students' perceptions and expectations when they make offers. This chapter shows you how to sell every step of the way and convert more applicants into excited interns and employees.

TIMING

In the minds of college students, as soon as an employer collects résumés, the clock is ticking: The "official" recruiting process has be-

> My top choice in the beginning of the process was a construction company that verbally promised a position. The lack of paperwork and follow-up, along with unreturned phone calls, forced me to continue interviewing and finally take a position with another company. Six months later when the company finally called back, they were annoyed to hear I accepted elsewhere. What was I supposed to do? Wait for them?
>
> —Abigail, science/engineering, MIT

gun and the expectation is that interviews and offers will soon fol-low. When employers wait too long after gathering résumés to con-duct interviews, they lose recruits.

Although few employers wait as long as six months between col-lecting résumés and conducting interviews, many lose recruits in only four to six weeks of downtime. More than 20 percent of the students in the MIT UPOP program accept offers from other em-ployers when their first-choice companies do not get back to them within six weeks of an interview. And even if recruits don't sign with competing employers, they become less excited about the prospects of working for you when you drag the process out.

Not only do some employers move too slowly, many actually start the recruiting process at just the wrong time. A Silicon Valley–based technology firm, for example, wasn't landing any full-time hires from Columbia University, a school they avidly tar-geted. In the firm's third year recruiting at Columbia, only three students applied for the company's eighteen interview slots, and, naturally, those three students weren't the strongest candidates in the class. The problem was that the company kept trying to recruit at Columbia in late March. Had they recruited in the fall, when top candidates are actively paying attention to companies visiting campus, the tech firm would have seen dramatically different results.

The screening process needs to start at the right time and run like clockwork. We recommend the following schedule. Remember that the deeper you move into the process, the faster you need to move.

Résumé collection to first interview	2 to 4 weeks
First interview to second interview	2 to 3 weeks
Second/final interview to extending offer	1 to 2 weeks
Total time from receiving résumés to extending offers	5 to 9 weeks

Recruiting for a full-time position

START	FINISH
Early fall semester	Before winter break (usually December)
Early spring semester	Before spring break (usually March)

Recruiting for an internship

START	FINISH
Late fall semester	Before spring break
Near (before) spring break	At least three weeks before end of spring term

Deloitte Consulting has been known to conduct first- and second-round interviews and get back to students within a week. This lets students know that the company knows what it's doing and knows what it wants in potential new hires. Like most professional services firms, Deloitte can more easily manage a shorter recruiting process than a manufacturing company because Deloitte hires entire classes of entry-level consultants all at once. They don't have to match each student with a specific manufacturing group, and it's easier to forecast the firmwide need for college hires because those hires will all be performing the same job. But a company like General Motors, which requires new hires to fill very specific roles in different groups, still needs to wrap up its recruiting process in fewer than nine weeks. All it takes is planning and creativity.

If you need to fill various spots in specific divisions, start your process only when you know exactly which groups are hiring, even if it means starting your process a little later. Starting later and running an efficient process is better than getting students' attention early on but losing that attention down the road. Or adopt the professional service firms' model of recruiting an entire class of new hires and then placing them later. Applied Materials hires new graduates into a rotation program in which they experience work in several groups over two years. Not only does this relieve the burden of making particular matches early on, but it gives students an opportunity to try and learn new things on the job.

Being creative to speed your recruiting is one thing, but be wary of taking it to the extreme. When employers find themselves needing a lot of talent in a short time, they sometimes skip the screening process entirely. When a shrinking supply of computer programming grads caught software development firms shorthanded just as the market was picking up, four firms made blanket offers to students at a couple of top schools: "If you'd like to come work for us, we have a spot for you." The employers couldn't have made a worse move. Students *like* the feeling of making it through a recruiting process, of *earning* a job offer over some of their peers. It doesn't seem very glamorous or competitive when employers offer jobs without even first meeting the students. As one Stanford junior said, "It makes the company seem desperate." Unless you want the buzz on campus to be that you can be everyone's backup employer because you'll take anyone, you have to at least pretend to evaluate students and tell them you'll get back to them a few days later.

THE ON-CAMPUS INTERVIEW

Many employers approach first-round on-campus interviews as their chance to weed out the applicant pools rather than to excite the best candidates for final-round interviews. Big mistake. That negative attitude, coupled with the traditionally short interview, often turns off the best candidates.

Many students complain that on-campus interviews are impersonal and disorganized, and that the interviewers seem uninterested or unprofessional. Often the representatives that employers send to campus have been dragged into the recruiting role at the last minute, just because they happened to be available that day.

The best recruiting companies approach on-campus interviews as a part of the recruiting process that is as valuable as any other. They take the following six steps to accomplish their goal of quickly evaluating candidates while continuing to impress and excite them about working for their organizations.

Engage candidates before the interview

Bain & Company calls candidates before first-round interviews to congratulate the students on receiving interviews and to set expectations for the meetings. The students are always excited by this extra attention and appreciate the firm letting them know ahead of time what will and won't happen. For example, if you won't have time for students to ask questions at the end of first-round interviews, this "pre-call" is when you let them know that and invite them to have a question-and-answer discussion by phone after the first round. This small gesture goes a long way. The pre-calls only take a few minutes each, and when divided among the firm's junior analysts, no one person has to make more than a handful. It's also another opportunity for an employee to assess a candidate.

Alternatively, consider hosting an event the night before first-round interviews. Students love the chance for more in-person contact with people from your organization, and you get the chance to evaluate students in a more natural, informal setting. Plus, the more contact you have with your prospects, the more likely they will show up to their interviews as scheduled.

Be ready for your interview

Students evaluate you as much as you evaluate them. Be ready to tell recruits about yourself, about how you started and how long you've been with your organization, and what your role is in the company's new-hire program. Also, be prepared to answer the following questions:

- Why do you like working at the company?
- What has been your career path there, and where do you see it going in the future?
- Why should I work for your company? (Read: What will I get out of working there?)
- What are some typical career paths for new hires?

At an interview for an internship with Schlumberger, the recruiter brought his bag of gear from the field, including hard hat, coveralls, and steel-toed work boots. It made the prospect of working for Schlumberger much more real and gave me a sense of where many employees start—dirty and working to troubleshoot problems with oil drilling rigs, but loving the adventure their job provides.

—James, science/engineering, MIT

Let students ask questions

Even if you are extremely pressed for time, let students ask at least one question and then show you care enough to provide a meaningful answer. If you are confident that you've attracted the right students at this point in the recruiting process, consider cutting down the total number of interviews you do and lengthening each interview time by 15 minutes so that the interview lasts 45 minutes. Let students know that you're devoting that extra 15 minutes to discussing whatever they wish. The extra time gives you more opportunity to sell candidates on your organization's best qualities.

Sell publicly, evaluate privately

It's good practice to not let the candidate know what you're thinking of her (especially if she isn't doing well) during the interview.

Some employers think they have to be overly tough during the interview process to show students that they are competitive and want only the best people. But there is a big difference between asking tough questions, which is perfectly fine, and demoralizing students who give you less-than-stellar answers. Students will know that your process is competitive when they discover that only three candidates of the seventy people you interviewed made it to the next round. And most students know when they are not doing well in the interview. So wait until you are behind closed doors to evaluate candidates, because treating them poorly in the interview will make you the subject of negative gossip all over campus. It will give you a reputation for being unfair or unpleasant and will deter future applicants from approaching your company.

Manage students' expectations

Your recruits want to be 100 percent sure they know how your interview process works. Tell them how many interviews are required at each step, when and how you will let them know your decisions (Will an HR rep or the interviewer call or send e-mail?), and any next steps they must take to continue the recruiting process with your organization.

Show common courtesy

Interviewers who get four-star ratings from students at the end of a recruiting season all do the following:

- Congratulate students on making it to whatever stage of the process they are in.
- Thank students for their time.
- Give students their business cards and welcome students' questions by e-mail.
- Convey enthusiasm for their own jobs.

Incredibly, so many employers forgo these pleasantries that students are shocked when they meet employers who get it right. Common courtesy requires little time or money but makes a big impact in your relationship with potential recruits.

ON-SITE FINAL-ROUND INTERVIEWS

If you are willing to invest the time and money for hotels, dining, and travel, the students you bring to your site for final-round interviews are probably strong candidates for your openings. In addition to a final round of vetting, your main goal should be to set yourself up so that when you extend offers, the candidates are more likely to accept them. You also want the candidates who ultimately don't receive offers to be excited enough about the visit to your company that they tell all their friends about just getting to make the trip.

Because it usually takes so little time to apply for jobs and because students figure they should explore all the options, many enter the recruiting process on a whim. The final-round interview stage is perhaps the first time recruits start to think of working for you as a real possibility. On the way to your site, students start to question everything: *What will I be doing at work? Would I enjoy living in this city?*

There are four main criteria your candidates use to evaluate you during on-site interviews:

1. **The people**

    Students can never get enough exposure to the people at your company because they have to decide whether those are the people they want to work with every day.

2. **The actual work**

    Students want to learn as much as possible about what the work will be like. They want to know what types of projects they may be on and what a person in their future role actually does on those projects.

3. The career path

Students want to know what a role at your company will do for their careers and, of course, what you do to actively support your employees' professional development—from mentoring programs to special training.

4. The life outside of work

Young recruits are looking for a place where there will always be enough people their age to hang out with. What will their social lives be like? Where will they meet new friends: At work? Outside of work? Is it expensive to live in the city?

To address those four areas of concern for students and to run a successful on-site interview, you need to do the following things.

Appoint a host for each candidate

Nothing makes candidates feel more comfortable and welcome while visiting your company than knowing you have designated people to watch out for them. The host arranges everything for the visit and is the first person the candidate should call if anything goes wrong. Allow time for the candidate to meet the host informally since the better the host gets to know the candidate, the more likely the candidate will share his or her honest concerns about joining the organization. Hosts do not necessarily need to be from human resources; choose hosts from any part of the organization as long as you think they will get along well with particular candidates and will take the host role seriously.

Make the logistics as smooth as possible

Students appreciate when the recruiting company does all the planning for flights, hotels, and transportation. Candidates also respond well to easy reimbursement procedures. These candidates are still college students: Even if you ask them to plan their own travel, you should at least give them a cheat sheet or a list of suggestions and tips. The more support you give them, the better off they will be, and gestures as small as an upgrade from a taxi to a car can really wow them.

Host a dinner or reception the night before

A division of Thomson West hosts a dinner the night before final-round interviews at a chic restaurant in Minneapolis. The candidates talk about their experience for weeks after they return to their campuses. Dinner out allows you to show off your city, but you don't have to leave your office if you don't want to. Gemini Consulting used to host a nicely catered dinner at the office the night before final-round interviews. The candidates got a feel for the office during an informal event while all the interviewers really appreciated not having to travel to a restaurant. Because more consultants participated in the evening event, the college recruiting team had more help in selling the prospects on the company.

Some companies prefer to have the host take a student out to dinner one-on-one. That works, too, but having all the candidates together eases any concerns students may have about the social life.

Make sure at least one of the interviews is with a senior person

Meeting some of the most important people in your organization will make your recruits feel more important themselves. Students seem to never stop talking about when they got to meet a vice president or director of a division. The candidate doesn't need to know that this senior person might have only as much say in the hiring process as an entry-level employee. If the students are enamored with the fancy titles, use it to your advantage.

Work

Investment banks and trading firms usually show students a trading floor in action, but every company can show candidates something in motion, even if it's only loosely related to the actual work the hires will be doing. Showing real work getting done is one area in which manufacturing companies have an advantage over their professional services counterparts. Even if a candidate is going to be designing just a small component of a new product, getting to see the manufacturing process helps convince any recruit that they are contributing to something big and real.

Introduce candidates to as many great people as possible

Think of employees who will really connect with certain candidates based on career goals and interests or personal and professional backgrounds. You want to keep tabs on who seems to connect well with each candidate because you will need their support when it comes time to get the candidate to accept your offer. At the very least, you want the candidates to have quality conversations with three company representatives in addition to the host and the interviewers. One of the three people should be relatively senior and one of them should be a peer, perhaps a new hire from the previous year who can offer another young person's perspective on career paths within the company.

Show candidates a bit of life outside work

While having your candidates stay at the airport Hilton may be convenient for you, it certainly won't get candidates excited about living in your city. Exxon commonly has final-round candidates stay overnight in a hotel in the Galleria area of Houston rather than near their core operations in refinery towns on the outskirts of the city. Medtronic has all their summer interns live near downtown Minneapolis rather than in the suburbs where the company headquarters is.

Set expectations about next steps and follow through

If you like these candidates enough to fly them to your city and rearrange your company's daily activities to make them feel welcome, add to your goodwill by setting clear expectations on next steps and by following through exactly as you have promised. If you say you will notify students in a week, call them in a week. If there is a delay, call them when you promised and explain what's up.

Send them off in style

You want every candidate to have a great last impression of you. Instead of letting candidates find their way out of your company alone after their final interviews, have the hosts check in with candidates when they leave to say good-bye and give proper closure to the visit. Good-byes are also a way to get a reading on how the candidates feel about the visit and the interviews and how likely they are to accept offers if you extend them.

MAKING OFFERS

John had everything a communications company was looking for, and he thought the company was really great, too. As the weeks passed after the final-round interview, John followed up with the company several times to reiterate his interest and to ask about next steps. Company representatives told John to be patient. As John's confidence in receiving an offer waned, he applied to and interviewed with other employers.

A financial services firm interviewed John and quickly made him an offer. One of the firm's most senior officers called John to say that, given how impressive the interviewers said John was, he really wanted John to join the team. Several other company representatives who had met John during the recruiting process also called to congratulate him and to reiterate how much they hoped to work with him. They even invited John to lunch so they could discuss any further questions or concerns John might have had.

Two days after John received the offer from the finance firm, he finally got one from the communications company, but in a much more disorganized and unprofessional way. He got a call from someone in human resources with whom he had not previously spoken. She said he had two days to fill out the official work application and turn in a few other supporting materials. "The HR person sounded so rushed and stressed on the phone," John reported, "I felt bad asking any questions and I didn't really get the chance to fully explain that I was considering another offer."

When John called the person from the communications company who had interviewed him (and would be his boss) to ask questions, the interviewer said that human resources would be handling everything going forward. So John called human resources with a list of questions, but they didn't return his call. Two days later, John's potential boss called and demanded a final decision. When John explained that he didn't get a call back from HR and still didn't even know what his compensation would be, the interviewer finally realized that he and his company had made a big mistake. But it was too late. John declined their offer and went with the financial services firm.

If you've invested so much time, effort, and money into identifying, attracting, and screening potential recruits, you don't want to fail in the last mile. The following tactics—employed by the Microsofts, McKinseys, and Goldmans of recruiting—make students feel like they've won the lottery when they receive an offer from you.

When you make an offer, give a good ego massage as well

The primary purpose of the first call is to let a candidate know you are making an offer, but use the opportunity to make a lasting, positive impression, too. Up to this point, you have maintained your guard and not let top candidates know how much you want them on your team, but now that the cat's out of the bag, you can shower them with affection. Let students know how much you really want them. Make sure the call comes from someone the student has actually met, and the more senior the person, the better. Leave the logistical details out for now, but schedule a call to discuss them later. With any luck, the candidate is too excited to focus on details now anyway and just wants to get on the horn to friends and family.

Get others to join in the wooing

Have anyone who met the student make a quick call to deliver congratulations on the offer.

The interview process is so stressful. The congratulatory phone calls really made me feel as though it was all worth it, like the company really wanted me.

—Sven, recent MIT graduate

A call from the candidate's potential manager goes a long way, and any big shots in your organization should make a quick call, even if they didn't meet the candidate. One heavily recruited Harvard senior said she chose Merrill Lynch over several arguably more prestigious banks when she got a call from an executive in Hong Kong whom she told her interviewers she had long admired: "He made me feel like I had a great future in his company."

We recommend making five to seven calls, maybe fewer, maybe more, depending on how many people really connected with the student during the recruiting process. Just don't go overboard. One Stanford student received 15 congratulatory phone calls from an investment bank after the company made him an offer. As it was recruiting high season, the student was on planes and not able to take most of the calls. Returning calls wasn't easy either as most of the vice presidents were out of the office when he called back, but he managed to get about half of the calls returned. A few days later, the student received yet another call from the company and didn't answer. Unfortunately, that call was from the managing director, who said he was upset the student hadn't gotten back to everyone at the company. That afternoon, the student got an e-mail saying the company had reconsidered the offer of employment. Too many phone calls from a company can place a heavy and unnecessary burden on a prospective recruit.

Go over the offer details with a fine-tooth comb

Going over details with the recruit once the formal offer is made is critically important. Many employers rush to give students offers without figuring out the basics of compensation, location, and work project. Some employers tell candidates they will reveal the job details once the student accepts the offer, but this strategy does not work. Accepting a job offer is one of the most important decisions in the lives of college students, and they won't do it without good information.

Go over all the following with the candidate by phone and then confirm it in writing.

- Compensation—Salary, signing bonuses, performance bonuses, stock options, etc.
- Start date—It's important to explain why you've chosen a specific start date. Perhaps there is some training the student has to complete as a prerequisite to starting work, or perhaps the start date is flexible and the student would like to change it to

accommodate her schedule for transitioning from school's end to starting work.

- Location
- Position and title—Candidates may have been considered for a few different positions in different groups or divisions earlier in the recruiting process. Make sure they know exactly which they are being offered.
- Vacation and other benefits
- Offer expiration—You should give them a firm date by which the offer expires. We will discuss later how much time you should allow them.
- Contact—Let them know whom they should contact with questions or to give an answer. Make sure the candidates know they aren't alone in the decision-making process. Give them the names and contact information of people they can talk with to get as much information as they need to assist in their decision. And be very clear about what they must do to officially accept or reject your offer.

WHAT STUDENTS ARE THINKING

Soon after candidates receive your offers and congratulatory calls, reality sets in and they begin to seriously evaluate their options. They contact their parents, older siblings, friends, professors, internship program staff, and career counselors. Often, the more they discuss the situation, the more their outlook can change.

Some students simply consider the work that they'll be doing, how working for your company can help their career, and what life will be like inside and outside the office. But other students start to freak out. The idea of leaving school weighs heavily on their minds, and the fear of the unknown gives them cold feet. They worry about moving to a new city. They worry about whether they're even pursuing the right career path at all.

Students congregate and talk about how much they hate having to decide on a full-time job offer because it seems so final: "This is going to affect the rest of my life." "How can the company only give me three weeks to decide?" Or, "How am I supposed to know if I want to do this the rest of my life?" Conveying the message early on that taking a position with your organization does not limit students' future career options is critical. And you might have to reiterate that message after you make offers, too.

> I received an offer to work in the investment banking group at Morgan Stanley and an offer from Lehman Brothers to work in sales and trading. Although the day-to-day job duties were really different, I really liked both jobs and companies and was completely torn. I really didn't know which job and career path was best for me. But after the managing director who offered me the position at Morgan Stanley told me that if things didn't work out that he would personally make sure that I could get into a sales and trading group there, I was sold.
>
> —James, humanities, MIT

Not all students will be nervous, however. For others, your job offer gives them new confidence. Before they get offers, many students are hard on themselves: *Nobody wants me. I am never going to get a job. I'll be happy just to get an offer.* Then, as soon as that first offer comes in (and it could be yours), the mind-set shifts to the opposite. If they said they dreaded interviewing before, now they love it. If they said they'd "take anything" before, now they try to leverage offers to force other employers to expedite their offers or to create a bidding war in hopes of getting more money. If they have one offer that is going to expire before a few others might come in, they usually will pass on the first one just like contestants do on *The Price Is Right*. They want so badly to see what else is out there that they'll pass on what's right in front of them. Because of the back-and-forth that goes on in students' heads, setting deadlines for candidates to accept or decline your offers is delicate business. We've found that the following offer expiration guidelines yield the best results:

	MINIMUM	MAXIMUM
Full-time offers in the fall	3 weeks	through winter break
Full-time offers in the spring	2 weeks	4 weeks
Summer internship offers in the fall	2 weeks	through winter break
Summer internship offers in the spring	1 week	2 weeks

Full-time offers usually deserve a longer decision period because they require a more serious commitment than internships, and it often takes a week or more for candidates to set up the meetings they may desire with people in your company before they decide. For students who get offers in the fall, allowing them winter break to decide gives them plenty of time to discuss their decisions with friends and family. But if your organization has problems staying in touch with candidates throughout the decision period, we'd recommend wrapping up fall offers long before the winter break so candidates don't forget about you.

Give candidates ample time to consider their offers but not so much time that they don't feel accountable to you or that they shop your offer to up the ante with other interested employers. Once you set a fair offer expiration deadline, give short extensions sparingly, on a case-by-case basis, and only for specific reasons, such as when a student wants to weigh two offers equally. If you have properly managed expectations throughout the process, students will respect you when you stick to your guns. When students ask employers for deadline extensions it's usually because they are waiting to hear back from other companies; however, many students ask for an extension because the employers haven't stayed in consistent contact and provided all the information the students need.

To minimize problems with extensions and to maximize your chances of getting highly desirable recruits, consider offering incentives for students to accept your offers by certain deadlines. One major energy company gives a $2,000 signing bonus to students who accept their full-time offers before a certain date. If you can't offer monetary incentives, offer an extra week of vacation during the first year of work, a choice of which group to work in, or an invitation to a special meeting or conference that new hires traditionally wouldn't get to attend. Even if the candidate is one you are willing to bend over backward to get, you're better off granting incentives than an infinite extension. Unless you are McKinsey, Microsoft, or Google, candidates rarely become signers after they're granted indefinite extensions, because months later, when time's running out on the other offers they've drummed up, they usually commit to the company who's made the last good impression on them.

To further minimize problems with extensions, you should leverage support from on-campus resources such as the staff of intern programs and career offices. These people provide one-on-one counseling to students as well as workshops on how to properly negotiate with companies for extensions on offers. Mark Sorenson-Wagner, director of the University of Minnesota's Career Center for Science and Engineering, says he often sees students ask for an extension from a company when they haven't yet interviewed with the company that they really want to work for. His office tries to enlighten students so that they see the process from the employer's perspective. Work with your liaisons on campus to educate students about what is and is not appropriate about asking for extensions with your company. You may also want to give workshops to students on how to handle the offer and acceptance process as well.

SALARY NEGOTIATION

Expect candidates to ask for more money, but if you want to avoid salary negotiations, then take a cue from the professional service firms. Accenture, Bain, and A.T. Kearney rarely grant requests for more money. They let students know during the interview process that every new hire is paid the same amount, and that the number is set by a market rate. As word about this practice passes from student to student, very few students request more money from these companies.

Other employers tell students they are willing to negotiate a raise once a student accepts an offer. This helps to avoid price wars with other employers because it forces students to make the first move. Keep your word if you use this tactic, or you will have a very unhappy new signer on your hands who may go elsewhere very soon.

"SELL" WEEKENDS

Investment banks and management consulting firms often invite candidates with offers to a "sell" weekend full of glamour and glitz. Typically, students arrive on a Friday morning, spend the day at the office, meeting everyone from people in HR to last year's new hires to senior executives. Candidates sit in on conference calls with clients or sometimes even face-to-face meetings, depending on how well the client understands or accepts taking part in the college recruiting game.

The company provides lunch, workday-style, to show the prospective employees where they might eat on a normal day. In the early evening the company hosts a nice reception at the office before taking all the recruits to one of the best restaurants in town. They strategically pair specific employees with individual prospects (good "sell" matchups) and in the evening do scavenger hunts in limousines, take in Broadway shows, or hop the hottest clubs in town—whatever it takes to get the recruits thinking about how great life could be if they worked at that company.

At the end of the night (usually the very early morning) the prospective new hires return to a hip or extravagant hotel like the W, Ritz-Carlton, or Four Seasons. Saturday morning includes brunch, maybe a tour of the city, or even a meeting with a real estate agent to show candidates housing options.

> The sell weekend was a blast. Yes, I had to remind myself that I wouldn't be put up in the Four Seasons every weekend, but it helped sell me on the company and the city.
>
> —Charles, McKinsey new hire

A pull-out-all-the-stops sell weekend usually gets candidates to accept offers, but there are lower-cost alternatives. Offer a scaled-down version. To save on airfare and steep hotel bills, offer a reception and dinner for students in your area. If you have a significant number of prospects near another city, fly a couple of your top recruitment "salespeople" out for a mini–sell event away from the office. Show your prospects you care about them. You want them to associate your organization with having fun and having a sense of community, especially with other people their age.

Fortune 500 companies don't often have extravagant sell weekends because they're hiring so many people at once. But some of these companies at least allow prospects—once they've accepted offers—to take one trip on the company's dime to their future work location to find housing. Inviting all new hires to use this benefit on the same weekend creates a great opportunity for you to make candidates feel welcome and to help them start making friends. Even if candidates know this won't happen until after they accept your offers, it could influence their decision making because they are so attracted to employers who actively build community among their employees.

CELEBRATING ACCEPTED OFFERS

Your candidates have accepted your offers. Hooray! Many employers think this is the end of the recruiting process, but the work is far from over. Start proving to your prospects now that they made the right decision, to help reduce their apprehension about starting a new chapter of their lives. Celebrate their offers by doing the following:

1. Make more congratulatory calls—These should be even more exuberant than the postoffer calls since these people have actually signed with your company. Have several employees call, and make sure that the new hire's manager is one of them.

2. Meet in person—If the new hires are located near your office or an affiliate office, take them to lunch or invite them to whatever team dinners or events you might already have going on.

3. Send a gift basket and card—Maybe it's a care package for final exam week or a small gift that you know suits their interests. Whatever you think of, it's a simple way to make your organization seem classy and professional.

You can do whatever works for your organization, but the most important thing is to make sure the gesture is sincere. If a student receives a card in the mail signed by an HR staff member she has never really met, it will just seem tacky.

Finally, give credit where credit is due. Thank everyone who contributed to your recruiting efforts—people inside your organization and even your partners on campus. Give yourself a pat on the back for recruiting one or many talented new additions to your organization. Take time to relax, of course, but also consider throwing a party for your recruiting team. There's no reason you shouldn't treat your own loyal and talented people like rock stars for a night just as you did your prospects during the recruiting process.

❖ *Chapter Takeaway:* The process of conducting interviews and making offers is as much about selling your prospects on joining you as it is about evaluating who you want to hire. The keys to successfully making the sale are (a) proving you offer a complete job experience, which couples interesting, challenging work with a good time in and out of the office, (b) maintaining consistent contact so you can discover and address all of a prospect's concerns, and (c) asking your existing personnel to make your prospects feel wanted every step of the way.

7

The Long Honeymoon

College students joke about how life in the movie *Office Space* seems like paradise: Arrive late. Jaunt to the neighboring restaurant for a midmorning coffee break. Take lunch immediately afterward. Just complete a few TPS reports, which seem to have no purpose, and the boss is happy. But when students think seriously about their own careers, they want the opposite experience. They want work that impacts the world. They want to stretch themselves and their colleagues to do more than they did yesterday. They want to have fun inside and outside the office. This is exactly what you've promised and sold to your target recruits to get them to accept your offers. The most important stage of the recruiting process is now: delivering on your promise.

Microsoft and McKinsey don't seduce recruits only to leave them shaking their heads with disappointment and regret once they arrive at the office. The best companies deliver the experience they promise, which helps them keep the folks they work so hard to bring in. It also lays the groundwork for future successful recruiting efforts and creates satisfied employees.

The long honeymoon starts the minute your recruits accept your job offers and doesn't end until they leave your organization.

POSTOFFER MANAGEMENT: TURNING JOB SEEKERS INTO JOB DOERS

Students usually prefer to receive and accept offers early in the academic year, especially for full-time positions. This gives them time to work out the logistics of the biggest transition of their lives: leaving college and starting a first job. They find an apartment, sign a lease, perhaps buy a new car. But even though a student has accepted your offer, he is likely still nervous or anxious about that decision. For many top recruits during the dot-com bust, for example, accepting early offers turned out badly. Days before they were scheduled to start work, after not hearing from their employers for months, many received calls from companies who said they weren't able to hire the new class of recruits. "Sorry."

Students who have heard similar horror stories are wary that you may drop the same bomb on them. If you really do want your recruits to show up on day one, take the time to make their transitions smooth and worry-free. You maintained consistent contact with your recruits throughout the interview process; simply continue that practice once students have accepted your offers.

One MIT engineering student accepted an offer from a large technology company very early in the cycle and was promised that he would be able to pick the group that he would work with. The recruiter then did not contact the student for six weeks. After being prodded by the student, the recruiter finally arranged a telephone meeting, but then did not keep it. More than two months later, the student spoke to the recruiter, who told the student that he could no longer pick his group because it was now too late in the cycle. The young engineer now seriously regretted taking the offer in the first place.

You do not want a new hire harboring resentment for your company before he even starts. His negativity will spread to your other recruits. The following tips for postoffer management will ensure more positive results:

Set expectations with new hires as soon as they accept your offers

Tell them how much contact you will have with them before they start work. Let them know anything they must do before they start work and when they must do it. Having a plan and communicating it to your new hires will separate you from the many employers who leave their recruits in the dark. Setting and managing expectations is the easiest way to keep new hires from being nervous about the unknown—and spreading that nervousness around.

Make contact with new hires at least once a month before they start

Whether in person or by phone or e-mail, get in touch at least once a month between offer acceptance and first day on the job. Even if you have no official business to address, call to find out their progress in preparing for work. Have they secured housing and transportation? Do they have any questions or concerns?

Connect new hires with their managers at least once before they start work

The managers should welcome the new hires and inform them of which projects they will be working on. This is especially important if the manager didn't have much contact with the new hire earlier in the recruiting process.

Inform recruits about organizational changes before they arrive

Don't let recruits discover in the *Wall Street Journal* that their new division is being sold or divested or that the company is performing so poorly that there will be layoffs across the organization. Juan, a Harvard graduate, received an offer from a management consulting firm only to read in the *New York Times* that the company was in trouble financially and laying off consultants. Juan immediately tried to contact the people who recruited him but neither they nor the HR department returned his calls. Three weeks before he was supposed to start, HR finally called and rescinded the offer. To this day, Juan tells other students not to consider that company.

These days, students actively look for gossip about companies they're considering on blogs or Web sites like Vault.com and Wetfeet.com. Someone at the top of your organization, perhaps the CEO or a vice president of human resources, needs to think about the company reputation from the perspective of new hires. Be straight-shooting with new hires: Communicate the good, the bad, and the ugly.

Even if you can't discuss news before it's public, contact your recruits as soon as it is. Not contacting them will put them into a frenzy—as happened with Juan—and they may look for new jobs. At least acknowledge there are some organizational changes taking place and let them know you will contact them as soon as the details can be made known to them. Most important, indicate whether any of the changes may affect the future of new recruits. If, for example, a new hire thinks she is going to work for a certain manager and that manager leaves your organization, tell the new hire right away, not on her first day of work.

Introduce new hires to each other

If your recruits didn't meet each other earlier in the recruiting process, make sure to connect them now. Let them start developing a community of friends before they start to work. The more comfortable they are with their coworkers, the happier they will be about where they are. Also, recruits can often help each other with issues like housing and transportation.

Help recruits settle all issues, from big to small

Even if you can't provide answers or solutions directly, provide other resources that can. Spell out everything your recruits need to know, even what you think is obvious. Too many employers don't specify when and where recruits should report for work, or even what clothes they should wear, despite the students' attempts to find out those details. If you don't provide housing and transportation, give your recruits the same helpful advice you'd want if you were in their shoes and had to arrange where to live and how to get to and from work on your own.

Gemini Consulting was a model company for postoffer management. Gemini sent all new hires a monthly newsletter with company happenings and profiles of other incoming new hires. A consultant stayed in touch with each incoming recruit from the time an offer was accepted to the first day of work. The firm-appointed consultants made personal contact with designated recruits once a month, culminating in a call one week before the recruit's start date to answer any last-minute questions.

THE TOTAL WORK EXPERIENCE

Once your new hires arrive—ideally free from worry and full of excitement about what may come of their time with you—it's time to help them get some work done. Keep in mind the total work experience the new hires are seeking and give it to them—or many of your recruits will leave within the year.

Recruits want to make a genuine contribution to your organization's goals and achieve results that propel their careers. But new hires evaluate both life on the inside and life on the outside of your organization, in addition to the work. How you perform in these three areas makes all the difference in whether new hires stay with your team.

THE WORK

The quality of the actual work is the number one complaint among young recruits surveyed about internships and first jobs. The reason? If not sufficiently challenged, a top recruit from a top-flight college starts to think of his first position as a demotion from what he's used to.

The curriculum at most colleges, whether a school of liberal arts, business, science, or engineering, is designed to teach students how to dissect, analyze, and solve open-ended problems. By the end of senior year, the best students are completing very rigorous projects. Business majors redefine marketing strategies for local businesses or start their own companies. Engineering majors design underwater vehicles and autonomous helicopters with swarm capabilities for the military. English majors publish articles, novels, and travel books.

Many colleges require capstone courses, in which senior students define their own projects, conceive the big picture, determine streams of work, and make all the critical decisions. At the end of senior year, students present and defend their work to a panel of professors and sometimes even real clients, such as municipal governments, non-profit organizations, and for-profit companies.

A software engineering graduate who is asked to do basic testing of your computer programs, a journalism graduate who is asked to copyedit, or a business school graduate who is asked to be an Excel spreadsheet data monkey will view their first jobs as grunt work. Of course, no college student or recent grad can realistically expect to set direction and strategy for your entire organization, but interns and full-timers still want to feel challenged, productive, and committed. Take the time to incorporate appealing attributes in their assignments, and they won't mind doing some grunt work along the way. Ask yourself the following questions when giving work assignments to young talent:

Is the work real?

Many new hires have nothing to do for weeks or months after arriving on the job. Sometimes the problem is a manager who doesn't feel he has time to arrange a meaningful assignment. He's too busy with the work he's already managing. Often, the new guy is assigned a number of articles and books to read in preparation for a great project that is supposedly starting in a few months. There are two problems with this approach: (1) There is only so much "background" reading material anyone can wade through; and (2) inevitably, projects get pushed back because of administrative glitches, and your young talent is stalled even longer.

While it is nearly impossible to align the start of an exciting project with a new hire's start date, it's even harder to coordinate projects for interns around your employees' summer vacations. This doesn't mean you're off the hook. If no good project is going to start for months after the recruit arrives, loan your new hire out to another group or have her work on a project that has been sitting on your back burner—something you always thought would be nice to have done but just didn't have the time to pick up.

Don't waste your new hire's energy and enthusiasm. Give him real work to do from the beginning. For full-time hires, the timing for assignments depends on formal training schedules, job shadowing, and rotation cycles. Try to have full-time new hires into a project within one month of the end of those initial activities.

And for 12-week summer internships, have interns fully engaged in a project by week 3. Any delay beyond that makes them lose confidence in you, and they will not take the experience as seriously as you'd like. If you have a superstar on your hands, she might even have found a great assignment with a competing internal group.

Is there a stream of work, even a small one, that the new hire can own?

A new hire will feel a vote of confidence from you if you give her a stream of work for which she can be ultimately responsible. The responsibility that comes with owning a project also raises the intensity of her work environment and, with that, her performance.

New hires can and should be part of a team, but they also want more accountability and independence than they get from simply supporting others. If you can't let a new hire own a stream of work when he or she first starts, build up to it as quickly as possible.

Does the work really matter or can we at least *make* it matter?

The answer to this question is subjective. One new hire may appreciate the importance of a project while another may never understand it. Don't count on your recruits to see the best of every situation. Prove to them that their work matters.

Chris, a finance and marketing major, interned at an asset management firm the summer after his sophomore year. His manager asked him to research the correlation between the spot prices of natural gas, petroleum, and coal, but Chris couldn't get a sense of where his research was going. The initial instructions were ambiguous and no guidance was provided. Chris had update meetings with his manager and he remembered his boss mentioning a short internal report needing to be developed, but this was said in passing. Finally, two weeks before the end of the internship, Chris began to have daily meetings with his manager to agree on the scope for what was going to be a seven-page report that would be distributed to the firm's investment personnel. Only then did Chris realize that his assignment was one of the most important assignments given to all the interns.

New hires who are on projects that are core to your business will stay excited about their work. Many employers claim they cannot put new hires in mission-critical roles, but there's always an opportunity for compromise. In engineering settings, for example, a new hire might not have the technical expertise to contribute to the core design of a new device, but consider letting her lead the writing of the technical manual to teach a client how to use it. And while it's often not appropriate for a new hire to represent the firm to clients, you might put her in charge of producing research summaries to help the sales team better prepare to engage new prospects.

If your new hires are relegated to support roles, let them know why their work is important. Who depends on the work and why? How does the department benefit? What happens to the company without it? One UBS intern was given an interesting, open-ended assignment to estimate the size of a market for a new business. The project was supposed to take a few weeks and required some complex data analysis and business sense. At the outset, the intern was excited, raving about the intellectual stimulation and new knowledge he was getting from the project. By the end, without further attention from the manager, he had lost all interest, complaining that his work probably wouldn't matter. But when he delivered the results, his boss was thrilled with the quality and quantity of work. Once the manager finally relayed to the intern the importance of the project, the student worked harder the rest of the summer. To this day, the intern actively recruits on behalf of the organization.

While a 15-minute conversation is often all that's needed, it's better if the manager engages the intern or new hire consistently throughout the project. Schedule a quick meeting once a week to keep your recruit motivated and on track. If a manager is "too busy" for updates, your recruit will conclude that the manager doesn't care and the work doesn't matter.

At the end of a project, let your recruit know how his contribution helped the project succeed. Everyone likes to be thanked and told how they helped to solve a problem. Interns and entry-level employees are no different.

Is the work assignment open-ended?

Open-ended projects require the recruit to generate new ideas and make decisions beyond simply following orders. "Open-ended" does *not* mean giving complete autonomy to your young talent. In fact, a manager on an open-ended project may need to be more involved than he is on a more straightforward one.

The Gordon and Betty Moore Foundation, for example, hired interns to find the most effective ways to monitor the conditions of a region in the Amazon River basin. The interns were given a specific technology and charged with figuring out how best to implement it. They debated which materials to use and how far apart to install monitoring stations. Had the lead scientist directed the recruits to build something to exact specifications, the project would not have been nearly as interesting.

Bain & Company allows new hires to consult as a team with local nonprofit organizations. The new hires take on project planning and strategy, which is more responsibility than they get on their normal projects, and the nonprofits benefit from the advice of the bright young consultants they couldn't otherwise afford.

Are your recruits learning a new skill or technique?

One new hire at a strategy consulting firm was given a special project in which he learned a statistical market research technique called conjoint analysis. Because only one other person in the firm knew the technique as well as he did, the young employee became the go-to guy every time another project team wanted to use it. The skill made the recruit feel useful and added luster to his résumé as well.

The skills learned by young talent don't have to be technical.

Oral presentation, writing, and teamwork may also be learned on the job, along with how to calm an unruly client or supplier and how to manage your manager. Reminding your new hires that these skills will advance their careers no matter what their future industries of choice will give them more appreciation for the work.

Is there variety in the work?

Nobody wants to do the same thing every day or the same type of project for years on end. No amount of selling the importance of the work will change this fact. But like the professor who tries not to graduate his PhD students, every manager feels the urge to keep a young person doing the same type of work for years to get a better return on his investment.

Keeping new hires on the same old task will hurt your organization's reputation with prospective recruits. Make a firmwide conscious effort to engage new hires in a variety of work experiences. McKinsey and other management consulting firms expect new college graduates to work only two to three years before moving on to the next stop on their career paths, whether it is to another place inside the firm, to graduate school, or to a job outside the firm. As a corollary, McKinsey accepts that it will have to retrain new hires often and regularly.

Scientific research companies are the biggest culprits for doing the opposite. Some seem set on never letting new hires out of the lab. Having good lab assistants and technicians is a key component of the research company's success, but not letting new hires appreciate work outside the lab will hurt the recruits' careers and the organization's reputation with future classes of recruits. Many recent graduates who work in labs look for new positions only months after starting their jobs. Often, it's not because they don't like the lab or believe in the work. They just want to be exposed to more than one thing.

Remember, college students and recent grads are young and still trying to figure out what their long-term career paths will look like. They need to be exposed to different things in order to discover the paths they like best. Management consulting firms have a natural advantage in that their projects change over every few months, but any organization can give new hires a rotation of small side projects so they experience a variety of work.

Exposing your new hires to new things doesn't always require that you give them side projects of real work. Invite new hires to sit in on meetings they don't normally have access to, like a strategy meeting with an executive team or a conference call with a customer. Recruits will enjoy the experience even as silent partners, and they will be thrilled to be asked for their opinions afterward. If you're lucky, their newcomer perspectives may even produce useful insights for you.

Will the new hire get significant credit or have something tangible to show for his work?

Talented young professionals want to feel special. They crave public credit or tangible products to share with their parents and friends. Patents, awards, publications, and special presentations are all great ways to fulfill your recruits' desire for credit for what they have contributed.

> I was so excited to see my name in the opening credits for the AND1 Street Ball video game I worked on.
>
> —Michelle, Black Ops Entertainment

Craig spent his time at Xerox mixing the same chemicals day in and day out. But once or twice a week, his manager invited him to join in the group's strategy sessions, even asking for Craig's opinions.

While his input may not have had any real value to Xerox, the meetings motivated Craig to work harder in the lab. Nearly a decade later, he still raves about his first position with Xerox.

DO THE SIMPLE THINGS RIGHT: COMMUNICATING AT KEY POINTS

Communicate well and consistently with your new hires. They will perform better, and your organization will benefit from the good marks received in the new hires' feedback to fellow students. Always check in with new hires at the start of a project, in regularly scheduled progress reports, and in project wrap-ups.

STARTING A PROJECT

To get the most out of your interns and new hires, take an hour at the start of projects to meet and discuss the following:

Project background
Explain first why the project is important, to whom it is important, how it fits within a larger project, and, ultimately, the organization's overall goals. Your new hires need to know this to buy in, before you give them the nitty-gritty details of what they have to do.

Your expectations
To this point in their lives, most new hires have existed in very structured environments: semester-long classes with a preset number of homework assignments and exams; sports tournaments and band competitions with well-known rules. Working in the real world, of course, is different. Changes may happen by the minute or may not happen for months at a time. Recruits slowly adjust to that

reality, but for the first few assignments, they need to know what you expect from them on multiple fronts.

- What are the goals of the assignment? What tasks take priority over others?
- What are the key deliverables? What must be delivered at milestones along the way?
- When are they expected to reach each milestone, and when will the project end?
- Who are the key internal and/or external people they will be working with? How do you expect the team to work together?
- What does a great job look like? Better yet, what does an A+ look like?
- How much time should they spend on particular streams of the project?
- Who should they ask for answers to routine, simple questions on a day-to-day basis to make sure the small obstacles of being new don't impede their progress?
- What is their budget, and do they need approval to spend?

The new hire's expectations

Wow your new hires by asking what their expectations are and if they have any requests or initial ideas about the project. *Listen carefully* and you will discover what interests them most about the project as well as any mental blocks they have about it that they might not otherwise voice until the block causes a major problem in the work. They may be eager to learn a certain skill or have direct contact with customers or play a bigger role in project update meetings. Whatever the requests, think about ways you might help them get what they want. You won't be able to fulfill all their wishes, but any attempt to grant just one will increase interest in the work. You will also earn loyalty when they see how you went out of your way to help.

Some new hires are afraid to voice their needs because they don't want to be a burden. Help them get over this fear by suggesting a few things you suspect they might want. When you can't meet their requests, make a note to consider the requests again when crafting future assignments. Anticipating and delivering on the wishes they have for their next roles will telegraph how much you value them.

PROGRESS REPORTS

For even a standard three-month project, have at least one formal progress meeting with your new hire. Get an update on how the work is progressing, but be prepared to give feedback on your new hire's performance—and to accept feedback on your own performance as a manager, too.

Go through the issues you covered in the start-up meeting, but what your young employees want to know most is whether they are on track to earn an A+ for the project (they love using the same performance labels from school). And if they are not on track for the A+, you need to tell them what they have to do to get there.

If your new hire's progress is subpar, deliver the negative feedback in a constructive yet direct manner. And do it at regular intervals so they have a chance to process it and act on it immediately to improve their performance. If you wait to deliver the feedback until the very end of an internship or during six-month or one-year performance reviews of full-time employment, your recruits will be upset that you didn't share your thoughts sooner and, defensively, spread word of your delinquency to their friends. And, of course, their fellow and former classmates will view the situation only through the eyes of your recruits.

During her first independent project for an oil and gas company in Texas, Sheila periodically asked her boss how she was doing. He always responded in a vague yet positive manner: "Oh, pretty good. Everything is fine." When the project was over and Sheila got her performance review, she got the equivalent of a B– or C+, not the A+ every new hire works for. Sheila did make some bad decisions, but she made those decisions at the start of the project. Had her manager addressed the problems directly and early, he would have gotten better results. He also would have prevented the negative gossip on Sheila's campus: "That stinks. It's totally not fair that your boss didn't tell you when you made a mistake. How were you supposed to know how to fix it?"

Finally, discuss whether you are meeting the new hire's expectations. If you promised the opportunity to sit in on important meetings or to learn a new skill and you don't think you are going to deliver, break the news now.

PROJECT WRAP-UPS

Look back on your start-up expectations and discuss whether they were met. Know, too, that this is the *last* chance you have to train behavior change in your new hire. Now is the time to talk through the minute details of the new hire's performance on the project. Do not save these details for a performance review in coming months.

The most talented people want to improve even more. Perhaps the nicest thing about training new hires is that they actually *can* be trained. Take advantage of this benefit of youth and address problems and bad habits now rather than later.

MANAGING THEIR CAREERS

Making the work of new hires seem challenging and exciting is important, but there's more to the care and feeding of your most talented recruits. You also have to manage the *careers* of the recruits in your organization.

In many organizations, employers let the work itself get in the way of caring for the careers of new hires. It's so easy to say that you are swamped and that pressing deadlines take priority over mentoring and other professional development activities. Employers also fear that developing the careers of their prized recruits contributes to new hires leaving the organization.

You can't afford to let either of these situations keep you from attending to your new hires' careers. You may gain productivity in the short term if you don't take time for career development, but you will also create disgruntled employees who will hate working for you and leave. Nothing drains productivity like resentment. Organizations that develop their people best are able to retain happy, motivated employees *longer* than their competitors.

When Deloitte Consulting was suffering high turnover, the firm established the Deloitte Career Connections (DCC) program to help employees identify other positions within the company that match their skills and interests. Employees have access to a Web site that offers assessment tools and one-on-one coaching. In three years the program has already saved the firm an estimated $80 million in staff replacements costs.

The career opportunities discussed in Chapter 1—rotation programs, job shadowing, seminars, and so on—are useless to your new hires without appropriate guidance and planning. Here's how to execute a comprehensive career care package.

CREATE A TWO-TIER MENTORING PROGRAM

Every new hire should have two mentors: (1) the manager mentor and (2) the company mentor.

The manager mentor is simply the new hire's normal manager, but to be a good manager, he must be a mentor as well. The manager mentor sees more of the new hire than anyone else and is most familiar with the new hire's strengths, weaknesses, interests, and goals. Structuring assignments so that new hires feel they are growing from the work while contributing to the organization's success is part of mentoring. In start-up meetings, progress reports, and wrap-up sessions, the manager mentor should keep the employee's individual career in mind as well. In addition to standard meetings that arise from the work, good manager mentors schedule informal mentoring conversations a couple of times per internship and about once a quarter during full-time employment.

The company mentor is someone who is senior enough to have responsibility for and visibility over several different parts of the organization. As the main link between the new recruit's manager, the recruit, and the rest of the company, the company mentor has honest conversations with the new hire about his career, including paths within the company that may be of interest to him but are also outside his current group.

The first conversation between the company mentor and the new hire should be about the new hire's goals and interests and each party's expectations for the mentoring relationship. By looking out for the best interest of both the company and the new hire, the company mentor must think about what's next for his mentee and how the organization can help him get there, monitor whether he is acquiring enough breadth and depth in his portfolio, and ensure that he is aware of what is going on with the company and the industry. The company mentor may recommend action steps for the new hire and the new hire's manager to work on together. A set of training classes, a new side project, or job-shadowing days are all activities that the mentor and mentee can arrange.

Finally, the more senior the company mentor, the more seriously the new hire's manager will take these recommendations. If the company mentor says, "It's not good that your new hire has been cooped up doing the same thing for the past year. This is what we need to do to keep him in the organization," the manager has to take action.

Mentors can also bring the expectations of new hires back in line with reality. For example, no matter how fast a new hire wants to advance her career, if it is unlikely that she will change departments in less than a year, the company mentor is the person to deliver that news.

Schlumberger's new hire program usually starts with an assignment on an oil rig. It's a tough gig and may last up to two years, but everyone knows that the oil rig project is necessary to rising through the ranks of certain parts of the organization. When new hires feel anxious to move on, the company mentor helps them understand that the policy exists for a good reason, or, if there is no good reason, the company mentor needs to candidly discuss that, too.

A formal 90-minute meeting between the company mentor and new hire should take place at least once a year. Beforehand, both parties must do their homework. To give the mentor a clear picture of his portfolio over the past year, the new hire should put in writing a list of his core projects and any special side projects, training classes, shadowing experiences, and one-on-one meetings with auxiliary mentors he has had in the last year. The mentee should also detail what type of skills, projects, or functions he would like to experience in the future.

This exercise also helps new hires gain appreciation for what they are already getting out of their jobs. Sometimes what *they* produce can be *your* most potent weapon in convincing new hires that they are getting a rich experience at the company.

Jenny and Sarah, two interns from MIT, went to work in the marketing department of a California-based life sciences company. Both were given the same type of market research and analysis assignments and they both received high marks from their managers on the quality of their work. Interestingly, each walked away with different opinions of the company. Jenny, who loved her experience and wanted to return full-time, had a manager—previously from McKinsey, by the way—who spent 30 minutes to an hour each week over coffee to discuss her work and explain why her assignment and experience at the company would truly benefit her career. Her manager also encouraged her to meet as many different people as possible throughout the organization. Jenny glowed about her positive experience: "I totally didn't know what I wanted to do with my life. My boss really helped me appreciate that I had so many options, and this was just a start."

Sarah, on the other hand, had a boss who barely spoke to her, and when he did, it was just to give her an assignment. It was clear he cared about the assignment, but it wasn't clear that he cared about her. The result: Sarah thought the work she did was pointless and boring.

CREATE A STRUCTURE THAT ENCOURAGES TALENT DEVELOPMENT

If you want your managers to take an active interest in developing the young talent you worked so hard to attract, give them incentive to do so. No matter how big your organization, there are probably enough opportunities for your most promising new hires to grow into, advancing their careers while benefiting your organization. Some organizations make movement automatic by implementing rotation programs. Others tell their managers that part of their performance evaluation is how well they develop their people. When you give managers incentive to get their new recruits ready for promotions to higher positions, they *will* do it.

Another way employers can foster the careers of new hires is to improve the coordination between HR and hiring managers. One medium-sized medical device company offers seminars at which new hires meet members of the executive team, practice running meetings more effectively, and learn more about specific products and the industry—all great perks for new hires. Unfortunately, few people attend the seminars. Some hiring managers thought the seminars took too much time away from work. Others left attendance up to their new hires, essentially guilting the subordinates into not attending for fear of disappointing their new managers. Had the managers and HR professionals who run the seminars communicated more effectively, HR might have realized that holding the seminars in the middle of the workday wasn't the best move, and the managers might have agreed in advance to send their people to at least a few more meetings.

ENCOURAGE (REQUIRE!) NEW HIRES TO GROW THEIR NETWORKS

Helping new hires make and strengthen relationships within the organization is one of the best things you can do for their individual careers and for their value to you as employees. Introduce them to your contacts in other groups and divisions. Tell them the protocol for reaching out to other employees in the company. Adopt "Take Your Manager to Lunch Week" and provide name tags for company social events to encourage introductions. You may even want to include in your formal list of expectations that your new hires get to know at least two new people outside of their working group each quarter. Make it clear that you care that they learn the different parts of your business and encourage them to make connections as a valuable part of development.

PERFORMANCE REVIEWS

Whatever your company's performance review process, consider the following tips to make it more effective—and conducive to keeping your young talent on board.

Make performance reviews more about the future and less about the past

An end-of-summer or annual performance review should not be the first time your new hire learns your honest opinion of his work. It's okay to use the time to document an aggregate of what you've already discussed in regular project progress reports and wrap-up meetings, but don't rehash every negative action from months ago. Assign a number or letter grade to their overall performance, but focus most of your effort on producing a plan to make the recruit a better employee in the future.

Whatever you spend the most time discussing is what your recruit will take from the meeting

Too many employers have alienated top-performing recruits because their performance review discussions were 90 percent negative, even though the overall quality of work, from the company's perspective, was positive. One manager from a Silicon Valley technology company defended this practice, saying he just liked to get to the point and if he didn't like the new hire he wouldn't be having a performance review. But your new hires will never understand that mentality.

Tim, for example, had a boss at an oil company who liked him but didn't spend much time with him. The boss was busy and pleased that Tim managed himself and produced good work, but he spent most of the end-of-summer performance review discussing Tim's weaknesses. At the end of the review, when the boss actually invited him to return the following summer, Tim was more than confused; he was ticked off. And, naturally, he declined the offer.

LIFE ON THE INSIDE

A vibrant company culture and community helps get top talent in the door, but it's even more important to retaining it. The best recruiters of young talent—Microsoft, McKinsey, Amazon.com, Goldman Sachs, Google, Apple, and so on—have many different flavors to their cultures, but they all boast a sense of community that's fun, energetic, and social. Google offers free food that employees love to gather around two or more times a day. They also have volleyball courts and a pool where their employees can play and work out. Employees and managers at a Boston-based software company break for an hour each day to play computer games against each other. This might not appeal to everyone, but it is a huge selling point to the most talented software developers.

At Microsoft, the flexible work environment allows for a group of employees to plan a hike on summer Friday afternoons. Many companies use community service projects to develop camaraderie, such as a charity golf tournament, a walk to fund breast cancer research, an elementary school tutoring program, or a canned-food drive.

Consulting firms like McKinsey and investment banks like Goldman Sachs don't have volleyball courts or swimming pools or "Wear Your Pajamas to Work" day. But they often cater lunches, sponsor drinks at a local bar, or hold dinners for new hires to make them feel a part of a community the minute they start to work. One Maryland-based private wealth management company sponsors an "Intern Olympics" every year in which the interns compete in a series of events, culminating in a song-and-dance contest.

Beyond the big events, simply how and where your people are seated in the office and what they usually do for lunch also matter a lot to young talent. A medical device company where everyone eats lunch at his desk and leaves at 5 P.M. is not going to attract an enthusiastic young engineer who wants to change the world. But one development group within that same company changed the configuration so that people working on the same projects can more easily share ideas and stories throughout the day. They eat lunch together and frequently plan social events. The group is known for working long hours, but it has no problem recruiting new hires because the group has created a fun place to work.

LIFE OUTSIDE WORK

No matter how well you manage your recruits' actual work situations and quality of life inside your organization, they won't stay with you for long if their lives outside the office are in a shambles. Housing, transportation, and recreation options matter.

It's impossible and impractical to serve as your new hires' full-time social planner outside of work, but you can start them out on the right foot in a new city. Sponsor a few events out of the office for new hires and other young employees to help them feel good about their social lives: sporting events, theater, hiking trips, museum tours, dinner and drinks at good restaurants. If your company is large, inviting people from different parts of the organization will encourage new hires to meet others outside their immediate working groups. If your company is small, host an event and let employees know to bring friends. You don't have to pay for everyone; organizing the event itself will suffice.

To battle the perception held by today's top graduates that "there's nothing to do" outside New York or San Francisco, employers in Minneapolis formed an alliance to organize recreational activities for summer interns and young talent. Former interns are eager to return for full-time work because the built-in community of young professionals eliminates their reservations about going to what some consider to be an undesirable location.

Housing and transportation are the two biggest logistical issues that interns and new hires have to deal with when starting work. You don't have to provide a suite at the Ritz and a Lincoln Town Car with a personal driver, but you can do a lot to ease young recruits' transition by just providing some good advice. If you provide corporate housing, use that as a selling point with recruits. If you do not offer housing, consider the following:

Reserve apartments for private lease. A group of companies in New Jersey arrange with a real estate company to make sure their recruits have first right of refusal on leasing apartment spaces. The employers are not involved in the actual leases, which are directly between the recruits and the real estate company, but they earn a dose of goodwill with their new hires by making it easy for them to find convenient housing in a new city. The apartments are great for social life, too, because the buildings are full of other young professionals.

Arrange for local real estate agents to show your recruits around. Show the recruits you care by setting them up with an agent you know and trust rather than letting them do their house hunting blind. We bet your agent friend won't mind the many direct referrals either.

Compile a brief, custom guide to the city. Provide a tip sheet showing which neighborhoods are nicest, which have affordable rent, and the transportation options that correspond to each.

❖ *Chapter Takeaway:* The management of new hires starts the moment they accept your offers and lasts until they stop working for you. It's time to deliver on all the promises you made while making the sale. Take care to always set expectations early. Communicate frequently to nip problems in the bud and show your concern for their development. Choose managers wisely and support them amply because those individuals embody the entire organization to new hires. And do whatever is in your power to help your newest employees enjoy life outside of work so they are happy and focused when they come to the office.

8

The Feedback Loop

The final piece of the recruiting machine, the feedback loop, is the part of recruiting that makes the process worthy of being called a machine at all. Feedback is taking a step back to learn from the past and using your new hires and all the prospects you've met along the way to make your next round of identifying and attracting talent a breeze. It's another way the best recruiting organizations separate themselves from the pack, because they execute the following tactics so diligently and so consistently that they improve how well they identify, attract, screen, and sign new recruits year after year.

GETTING YOUR REPORT CARD

At the end of Erica's internship at an electronics company, she and the other interns were taken out to dinner and asked to complete a two-page survey that would tell the company's campus recruiters what was good and bad, how orientation could be better, and so on. If we took you out to dinner for reading this book, what kind of feedback would you give us? Bet you'd be pretty nice. (Or no dessert for you!)

Recruiters often set themselves up for failure by using the wrong method to ask the wrong questions of the wrong people at the wrong time. Many organizations get data from interns at the end of the summer and from entry-level hires after six months or a year, but the feedback is usually all positive even when the company's conversion numbers are going down the tubes. This chapter shows you how to get *honest* feedback about your image, recruiting efforts, and your recruits' experiences on the job. And the first thing you need to know is that the only way to do it is without your recruits knowing!

One software company had a classic problem. Its recruiting machine seemed to be firing on all cylinders—all of the feedback about the company's recruiting process and interns' summer work experience was very positive—yet it couldn't convert summer interns from MIT into full-time hires once they graduated.

The head recruiter took three smart and rigorous steps to get to the bottom of the mystery: (1) she asked the staff who managed her company's internship programs and the interns' managers to pass along any discoveries from their normal, informal check-ins with students throughout the summer; (2) she called the MIT interns about three months after their internships ended (enough time for them to be emotionally separated from the company) and asked for their advice on how to recruit the next year's interns; (3) she talked to interns from other colleges who had worked closely with the MIT students during the summer. She then got the honest feedback she needed: The interns who weren't returning had thought their work was "boring." Now the recruiter has a fighting chance to correct the problem within her organization.

Simply having the right people gather information in the right way makes all the difference. The company's past interns wouldn't give the campus recruiter honest feedback in standard surveys because they had grown to like her so much as a person. They didn't want to write anything negative on a formal evaluation of her and of the company's recruiting efforts because they didn't want her to know what they said or cause harm to her career. By asking the intern program managers and the interns' direct managers, though, she got the candid information she wanted without the students worrying that she might see it.

When she did ask the interns for feedback directly, it was with the right questions at the right time. Students will give you more thoughtful and honest feedback three months after the internship than during a celebratory dinner at the end of the summer. (No need for a waiting period with full-time hires because they're already on your team. Engage them early and often.) By asking students for recruiting advice for the future rather than "How might I have improved last year?" you will get their thoughts on how you did last year blended with the best recruiting tactics they've seen or heard from other employers or friends.

Contacting the people who would have had the most intimate conversations with the MIT interns was smart, too. The interns from other schools yielded good results for this recruiter; talking with professors, career advisors, academic counselors, and student leaders on campus who have close relationships with your prospects is also a good bet.

Your ability to get honest feedback from any of those parties will depend on the strength of your relationships. Follow the advice of best-selling author and relationship expert Keith Ferrazzi, who says, "Build it before you need it." MIT UPOP staffer Liz Arnold concurs: "We have feedback and advice for almost every employer we deal with, but we only deliver it when we know them well enough to be confident that they'll receive it well and that our students' careers won't be jeopardized because of it."

Getting honest feedback is not easy, and you may not always uncover the truth, but make the effort and then remember to put the feedback you do get to good use. You'll stay ahead of the employers who don't seek feedback at all—and they do exist. You'll also beat the employers who get lots of feedback but don't act on it. When you do

188 | RECRUIT OR DIE

make improvements based on feedback you receive—such as ensuring your interns have really interesting work—be sure to tell your employees and your prospects. When they know for themselves you've acted on and corrected a problem, they will help you spread the word to future recruits.

TURNING EMPLOYEES AND PROSPECTS INTO EVANGELISTS AND SCOUTS

If you are graduating disgruntled prospects, interns, and full-time employees from your recruiting process and organization, you'll likely get back the same in future recruits—if indeed you get future recruits. If you treat interns, prospects, and new hires well and deliver on what you promise, their respect for your organization becomes your single best tool for recruiting future prospects. Send your happy campers on recruiting missions to their own schools, and stay in touch with great recruits as they go on to other jobs. When past interns and employees consider themselves alumni of your excellent First Job University, they will show infectious pride and support of your future recruiting efforts. Prospects who never even joined your company will also say nice things about you—if you play your cards right.

Jake remembers one particularly nice recruiter who called him about an internship. The recruiter described the company and invited Jake to a site visit. When Jake told the employer he didn't have a car and wouldn't be able to get to their location, the recruiter offered to pick him up. Jake was surprised and especially grateful that the employer had offered to drive him, since he'd taken the commuter rail to other interviews and wasted a lot of time. On the way to the site, the employer described some of the projects that Jake might work on and said that if Jake took the job that summer he could choose the project he liked best. Jake met many people that day and was impressed by the company culture.

In the end, Jake made the difficult decision to accept another offer that was better suited to his interests, but a couple of weeks later, when one of his friends was considering an offer from the company, Jake did not hesitate to tell the friend about the positive experience he had there. Happily, the friend quickly accepted the company's offer.

This was a small company, so its name didn't attract students as easily as some high-profile companies. But Jake and his friend were sold on the organization because it showed that they really cared about the recruits.

Enjoy the good fortune of a lost prospect doing some recruiting for you, but don't leave it to chance with your interns and full-time employees. Ask them and train them to help you find and sell the top talent.

General Electric Aviation employs one former intern as a student recruiter at each of its target campuses. "Employ" here does not only mean "use." GE Aviation actually pays the student to send e-mails to his friends and associates and to share his experience at company recruiting events on campus. Whenever people see him, they think of GE Aviation—he's a walking billboard for the company. You might think it would be great to get former interns to champion your cause for free, but given how small a stipend it takes to constitute "good money" to a college student, it is worth paying to make sure your student ambassadors treat your requests as responsibilities.

Many employers wouldn't dare use people so young to aid their recruiting efforts. At other companies, only employees in their third year or beyond are deemed knowledgeable enough about the organization and senior enough to evaluate talent. These companies are missing the boat.

First- and second-year employees are usually eager to help recruit because they are close enough to the process themselves to still be able to relate to it. Their up-to-date knowledge of their colleges'

USING TECHNOLOGY AS AN AID

What kind of technology do you need to help run your recruiting machine? It depends on the number of people you're recruiting, the number and types of points in your process, how many people will participate on your recruiting team, and how much money you have.

If you need to land only one talented recruit from a single university every other year, you can probably just use your current e-mail program and a paper notebook. If you're trying to reach hundreds or thousands of students at multiple universities nationwide, you may need a large-scale enterprise system. For every level in between, the technology you need is dictated by the recruiting tactics you choose.

- To record contact information and notes about prospects and campus partners you meet, use a Microsoft Excel spreadsheet, your e-mail program, or even the same customer relationship management (CRM) system your organization uses to manage its sales pipeline.
- For sending invitations and tracking RSVPs to recruiting events, use the free Web services of Evite or Goovite.
- Teach For America sends a "How come?" survey by e-mail to any applicant who drops out of their recruiting process. If you want to make a survey part of your recruiting machine, basic tools such as SurveyMonkey or Zoomerang enable online surveys for little cost.
- If you need something to collect and manage résumés, consider systems like RESUMate, askSam, or CVManager.

To run a large recruiting program with all these needs and more, you may require an end-to-end human resources system like those provided by Oracle PeopleSoft, SilkRoad technology, and Kronos. These companies have solutions for all parts of the recruiting and retention process: résumé collection, screening, status updates for applicants, hiring and training milestones, surveys, data analysis, and more. It's important to note, however, that even such fancy technology is only as good as the data you put into it, so before you buy, consider how you'll get all members of your extended recruiting team to use the system. The more notes and data they enter, the more assurance you will have that your organization owns and preserves significant knowledge from your recruiting campaigns rather than just relying on an individual recruiter keeping it in her own mind.

Regardless of any technology tools you use, here's one easy tactic to implement immediately: Set up an autoresponder in your e-mail program so that whenever a student sends you a message, she will be notified that you received her message. One of the most common complaints of students across the country is not hearing back from employers they have contacted and worrying that their messages have disappeared into a black hole. Rather than get hung up on technology for the sake of technology, look for ways to use technology to aid you with even the simplest human problems that arise in recruiting.

courses and new programs and clubs is valuable for evaluating résumés. You can also get younger employees to execute the guerrilla marketing tactics that a VP would never do: putting up flyers around campus, forwarding e-mails to student groups, and jockeying for the best campus space for your events.

If you don't think your young employees are ready to handle every aspect of recruiting, then train them. Make sure they watch your best recruiting salesperson give the new-hire presentation, and ask them to take notes on how he sells the company and his experience. Have them practice interviewing your current interviewers, and have those folks playing the student roles ask the toughest questions of your young employees. Many professional service firms actually have this training built into their two-year analyst programs.

REFILLING THE TALENT PIPELINE

The business truism "It costs less to keep a current customer than to find a new one" applies as much to recruiting as it does to sales. Keep your talent pipeline filled with the prospects you've evaluated in past recruiting cycles, and you can move past trying to attract "someone, anyone!" and on to extracting just the right new hires.

It's especially advantageous to reacquire talent you've previously had your hands on. One recruiter from the U.S. Department of Education met and was impressed by a recent graduate from the University of Oklahoma who was an intern on the 2004 Bush/Cheney presidential campaign. When the department was looking to hire, the recruiter called the Oklahoma grad several times to express interest and offered her a job fairly quickly after an interview. In another example, Westat, a statistical research firm, really liked the work of one summer intern from Stanford. After his internship, the humanities grad moved to Europe, where he planned to teach English in the Czech Republic. When he realized teaching wasn't for him, he moved back home, telling a friend from the internship (who told the internship supervisor) that he had moved back to the States but wasn't yet proactively looking for his next job. Still, his former supervisor called to say that if there wasn't a job opening, he'd see to it that they found one. That made an impression on the recruit, who ultimately accepted Westat's offer for full-time employment.

Of all your prospects for full-time positions, the ones who have interned with you and enjoyed their experience are the most likely to sign on, but you have to continue to sell them as we've discussed in earlier chapters. Maintain contact—at least a phone call or an e-mail once a month. Be prepared to give them more special treatment than a new recruit would get. A signing bonus for an offer accepted by a certain date is a standout gesture for a standout intern.

One marketing company got creative when competing with an ad agency and a large restaurant company for the services of a previous graphic design intern. Says the student, "I went with them because I interned there the longest and knew the people well. And they said they would buy me a brand-new Apple G5 computer if I came back. I think that did it." What's better than converting an intern to a full-time hire by buying equipment you'd soon upgrade to anyway?

Of course, you don't always want your past interns to return. You may have invested more in them than in other prospects, but you're really just paying for a chance to evaluate them further. If you are not completely happy with their performance, don't give them full-time offers. It's better to take only the best people (like Microsoft does) than to lower your standards just to boost your conversion numbers.

Manage your talent pipeline carefully, and you will continue to have access to former prospects. Interns are not the only ones you may not want to lose sight of. Prospects who might deserve a second look may have fallen out of your recruiting process at any of these three stages:

1. When you reject résumés
2. When you reject candidates after interviews
3. When recruits decline your offers

To maximize your chances of hiring prospects who may have been lost along the way, keep in mind the following:

- *The deeper into the process, the more personally delivered your rejection needs to be.* It's okay to notify a student in writing that her résumé didn't win her an interview, but when you turn someone away after an interview, a phone call is required. After first rounds, an HR representative can make the call. After second or final rounds, the call should be made by the person who interviewed the candidate.

- *If there's a chance you want a prospect back in the future, make it clear that you want them to apply again.* College students take rejections from employers like they're being dumped by a first love. They think it means that you are deeming them completely useless forever, and most develop strong defense mechanisms that tell them never to try working for your company again. You can break through by telling them to try again. Fortune 500 companies probably lose out on the most former prospects with future potential. Their applicant pools are so large that they can't possibly make the time to tell each individual something like "We're looking for these four things and you're just quite not there with X. If you work on that, we'd love to see you apply again."

This presents a big opportunity for smaller competitors because you can easily win favor with still-developing young talent by taking the time to give candidates who don't make the cut compliments on what they did well and talking about how they could improve their

---

My best interviewing experience was with Jet Propulsion Laboratories. I was a mere freshman when I interviewed, but the interviewer gave me a great deal of personal attention, and it was clear that he was interested in figuring out where I fit best in the company to benefit both parties. Too often I have had interviews where it was treated like a zero-sum game. I didn't get the job that time around, but I intend to keep applying there and at similar places until I do.

—Seth, aerospace engineering, Arizona State University

When a senator's office contacted me to say I didn't get the internship, they said there was an overwhelming number of applications and I was on a preferred waiting list. That was the best "negative news" I've ever heard. Even though I did not get the position, it was encouraging to know they actually looked at the application and might contact me again. It definitely makes me more likely to apply again.

—Kate, humanities, Stanford University

I applied for an internship at Microsoft a year earlier than they wanted. Although they turned down my application, they wrote that they would like to see me apply the following year. Showing they cared that I applied really impressed me.

—Ben, science/engineering, Stanford University

skills to eventually work for you in the future, rather than simply saying they can't work for you now.

It's also important to show some class when prospects reject your advances, because stories of employers being bullies or sore losers spread fast and furious on campus. Take the high road when a prospect declines your offer, and you may have a chance to bring that talented student into your organization in the future.

When a student rejects your offer for a summer internship, follow up during or after their summer internship with another employer to reiterate your interest. There's always a chance that they were not happy with their choice, at which point you may quickly become the employer they turn to next.

When a student declines your offer for an internship or a full-time job, the single best question you can ask them is: What can we do to get you to reconsider our offer? This question cuts to the core of the issues. It will help you uncover things that you can address and give you another chance to sign the talent you want most. When the answer is something that's out of your control (e.g., you're based in Wisconsin but the student wants to live in a tropical climate), then you know what details to make more clear at the outset to future recruits.

Last, but not least, ask prospects who declined your offer which employers they did choose. Their answers reveal who your competitors really are and help you keep tabs on the great young talent you've identified. You never know when the feedback loop will put those prospects back in the front end of your recruiting machine.

❖ *Chapter Takeaway:* Using a little creativity, establishing trusting relationships, and earning a reputation for acting on constructive criticism will help you get the honest feedback you need to improve your recruiting. If you use your interns and employees who are most enamored with your organization to spread that feeling to future recruits and keep track of all promising prospects—even those who dropped out of your process last time around—you can build a feedback loop that will transform your recruiting plans and activity into a powerful machine.

PART THREE

YOUR RECRUITING STRATEGY

A Successful Company Leads to
Good Recruiting, and Good Recruiting
Leads to a Successful Company

Now that you understand your target prospects and possess the operating manual for your recruiting machine, you need a strategy for putting all the pieces into play. Your first move is to evaluate your own organization's strengths and weaknesses (a 12-question assessment tool will help you fine-tune your company pitch). Next, you determine your specific recruiting goals, including the quality of recruits you're looking for; numbers of applicants, interviews, and hires; and a way to measure your progress toward those goals.

Once you define your recruiting goals, you need to galvanize your entire company to be on board. The most successful recruiters always have the strong support of everyone from the CEO through the HR department secretary. So be sure you have the right people on the home front to help carry out your mission.

One Fortune 500 company didn't look before leaping into recruiting at MIT and subsequently rang up a record of 16 consecutive offers turned down by its recruits. Finally, the company took a break to assess the damage and prepare a focused recruiting plan. Three years later, the company is back in the swing of things, getting results by approaching MIT like a small company would—targeting small student groups and campus influencers, and managing the process one relationship at a time. You can do this, too.

Microsoft and McKinsey are successful companies that recruit successfully, but they don't rest on their successful-company laurels when they recruit. Companies who know what it's like to have top talent join their ranks will do anything to keep the successful recruiting cycle in motion. Once you understand what top talent can do for your company, you can make sure you have the best people on task to recruit even *more* top talent.

9

Define Yourself and Your Goals

If you had only 30 seconds to write a personal ad about your organization that strikes a chord with prospects, what would it say? What is the message you want to send about the benefits of working for your company? Or, as Ed Michaels, Helen Handfield-Jones, and Beth Axelrod put it in *The War for Talent*, what is your "employee value proposition"? What is your "compelling answer to the question, 'Why would a highly talented person choose to work here?'"

To compete in the war for young talent, you must be able to reel off answers to those questions at a moment's notice. The best recruiting organizations have the most simple, powerful answers:

Microsoft: You'll work with the world's smartest people.
McKinsey: You'll be a carefully chosen member of an intelligent, elite army.
Google: You will get to change the world.

It's no surprise that even the two industries that seem to most consistently attract top talent possess similarly pointed hooks: investment banking (You will make a ton of money) and management consulting (You will be exposed to many different industries).

Granted, these organizations and industries have the benefit of messages that have been refined and ingrained into the memories of college students over the course of many years. But since the college student population is in constant flux, it is possible to gain some ground. The hardest part is first taking a good, hard look at who you really are.

One financial company looks to most people like a great place to work. The company has a clear promotion path, famously nice people, and great benefits, including tuition-paid educational sabbaticals and such a huge bonus after seven years of work that it makes spending a career there seem worthwhile to most. This company is also a pleasant suburban alternative to New York City's cutthroat financial district: same type of work day-to-day but with a more laid-back lifestyle and without the looming "up-or-out in three years" rule.

The problems arise when this company begins talking to prospective recruits and some of its people try to make the company seem just like a Wall Street firm. The result: They fail to appeal to the students who would prefer the company's unique offering to working on Wall Street, and the firm ends up in competition it can't possibly win for students destined for downtown Manhattan.

Like this organization, you need to honestly assess your strengths and weaknesses and sell the top two or three things that truly make your company special. It's better to be yourself, because if you try to be everything to everyone, you'll recruit no one.

SELF-ASSESSMENT: TWELVE QUESTIONS TO ASK YOURSELF

If we went blindfolded into a career fair, many employers would sound the same to us, saying things like "We offer a good career path," "It's a fun place to work," and "The work is exciting." Such vague statements aren't compelling enough to attract top talent. In fact, your most desired recruits are a bit skeptical of those words because most employers don't actually deliver on those promises. Ask yourself the following questions related to your company to find out what you really have to offer students:

Q: What do your organization's youngest employees brag about to their friends?

George has had plenty to brag about while earning an Ivy League degree and working two years at a top management consulting firm, but the most excited we've seen him is after a recent win in his new position with a nonprofit in Washington, D.C. He sent us (and everyone he knows) an e-mail the moment it was announced that his organization had received a $3.3 million philanthropic investment because of a new strategic plan that he helped to write. Not one cent was tacked on to his salary, but certainly a big bullet was added to his résumé, and great pride about contributing to something important swelled within him.

Q: What do you and your youngest employees complain about?

One of the quickest ways to honestly assess your organization's strengths and weaknesses is to think about how you describe it candidly to your family, friends, and professional contacts when you're not recruiting (even though we know you're really *always* recruiting).

Q: What are your organization's core values?

These are the beliefs and aspirations that guide everything your organization does. Every organization has values. Many even have them written down and mention them frequently. It's your job to keep these in mind for recruiting, too.

Q: If your own child were a new college graduate, would you recommend she work for your organization? Why?

We often meet hiring managers who desperately want summer interns who will return for future internships and full-time employment but who advise their own children to switch employers if necessary to explore as many options as possible.

If you don't think your organization provides enough opportunity for growth, mobility, and long-term fulfillment for your own child to spend a career there, then you can bet other talented prospects feel the same.

Q: What's the best thing your organization does for employees' career growth?

Working for a dog food company in the Midwest might not seem appealing to top talent from an elite school on the East Coast, but answering this question has helped that employer land new MIT graduates each of the last two years.

"Although our headquarters isn't in a big city, we are a global company that's owned by another global company, so we can offer a unique opportunity for new graduates to get global experience by transferring to another location or maybe even another subsidiary of our parent company," says their recruiting manager. "Coming to the middle of America is easier to stomach when prospects learn that our first MIT recruit is now working in Japan after 18 months with us."

Q: What are your recruits doing one, three, and five years down the road? Is this what you *want* them to be doing?

If your past new hires have moved on to new, exciting positions inside your organization or with other employers, or if they've matriculated to respected graduate schools, then you'll have great evidence to show prospects that you care for the careers of your recruits. But if they haven't gone on to truly bigger and better things, you'll need to make some changes to attract top talent in the future.

Q: What's the most common reason people give for leaving your organization?

If most people leave to take advantage of great opportunities that their time with you has better prepared them for, then this can be positive for your recruiting image. But if their reason is more to get away from you than to arrive somewhere else, you've got problems.

Q: What percentage of your organization's employees hangs out with coworkers outside work?

If the answer is very low firmwide, is there a particular division or group that has team spirit that lasts beyond 5 P.M.? If not, you may need to recruit more locally to ensure that your new hires enjoy their life outside work.

Q: What about your work environment makes it better than the one in the movie *Office Space*?

Most college graduates would rather die than work in a sea of cubicles where no one talks to each other and you can hear a pin drop on the floor.

Q: Do the work experiences you provide interns and entry-level hires actually match what you've promised in the past?

Some financial services firms lose new hires after only six months or a year because they overpromised how intellectually stimulating the actual work would be. Often new hires who decide to sign on for that reason leave when they discover that most of their job is a mind-numbing routine of building spreadsheets. In cases where the work may be less than scintillating, firms will land better-fitting and longer-lasting recruits by selling their intense environments and the potential for great compensation.

Q: How often do your new hires change projects?

Management consulting firms can say that they will expose new hires to many different industries because project engagements typically last only a couple of months. If your business is different, you'll have to describe the work experience differently.

Q: How much do new hires really contribute to the critical decisions affecting the manufacture of your products or the delivery of your services?

Any new hire would love to step in and be CEO or lead designer on the first day. But new college grads will be happy with less if you offer ways to help them learn new ideas and build skills to advance their careers. Problems arise, however, when, say, engineering firms producing big, complicated machines like airplanes or engines promise recruits truly innovative work. When the new hires realize soon after coming on board that they need 10 to 15 years' experience and expertise to really call any design shots, they become very discouraged. It's better to be honest about the realities of your industry and more boldly proclaim the benefits you *can* deliver. Perhaps your new hires will learn from the best in the business as they work alongside industry veterans, and that is what they need to become star players later in their careers.

ANSWER THESE QUESTIONS honestly, and you'll know what you are and what you're not, and thus how and how not to present yourself to prospects. Knowing yourself well will also help you more effectively focus your recruiting efforts, wasting less time struggling to make relationships work with students who probably won't work out as valuable long-term employees.

The college recruiting team at a multinational technology company has a deep knowledge of their organization's strengths and weaknesses and applies them impressively to guide their efforts. For example, they recruit MIT students to work in some business units in Germany but not in the same groups in the United States.

"MIT students are looking for work that's new and different and intellectually stimulating. A lot of what we're offering is business engineering jobs. The challenges are with processes and management, not necessarily the innovation of a new product," said one recruiter.

The chance to live in Germany is an extra dimension that turns those jobs into wholly satisfying experiences for some students, but for MIT students who want to work in the United States, the firm recruits only for their research and life sciences divisions. "I'm sure there are a few students who would enjoy our core functions in the U.S., but it will take longer to find them than we'd like to spend," the recruiter added.

That's real recruiting strategy: knowing what you have to offer and making tough decisions to best match those offerings with the recruits you want most.

DEFINING YOUR TARGET RECRUIT

After determining who you are, the challenge is to decide who you want to recruit. The best recruiting companies focus on finding prospects who possess specific values and talents (inherent qualities that you can't change) more than specific skills or knowledge (things you can teach and develop).

McKinsey, for instance, hires many people with no previous business background. They are more interested in a prospect's raw intelligence, entrepreneurial spirit, and ability to think in a structured way. McKinsey believes that if it can recruit people with those qualities, it can teach all the necessary business vocabulary, principles, and skills on the job.

Microsoft first and foremost looks for a remarkable passion for technology in their recruits and an appetite for solving hard problems. Of course, those aren't the only values and talents an employer can look for. Maybe you'd like to see great work ethic, creativity, initiative, leadership, or something else altogether. On its Web site, Goldman Sachs lists and describes the following six attributes it wants in new hires:

- A passion for excellence
- Belief in the power of the group
- Integrity
- Leadership
- A desire to be challenged
- The drive to make your mark on the world

It's valuable to articulate the major qualities you're seeking in a recruit, but it's even more useful to narrow them down to the top two or three that matter most. It's a challenge, but doing so will make you more focused and make it easy for everyone in your organization to remember.

Denver-based EchoStar, creator of the DISH satellite television network, has done exactly this. The traits it looks for first in a recruit are energy, need for achievement, and intelligence. "We determined those to be the three things people need most to succeed at EchoStar," said college recruiting manager Angela Heyroth. "So no matter if we're hiring for entry-level or HR or a vice president position, that's what we look for first."

Placing such importance on talents doesn't mean these employers are hiring unskilled people. Skills are what they evaluate next, but even then they aren't too picky. Companies often evaluate skills with a talent mind-set. If a prospect has an amazing gift for solving computer problems, Microsoft won't ding him because the specific code language being used on a project isn't also on the prospect's résumé. It knows that the most talented recruits learn quickly.

Unfortunately, some employers take a much more short-term, narrow-minded, and harmful approach. We've seen students who are at the top of classes that require design drawings to be done in AutoCAD get turned away by employers who use only ProEngineer, a similar program. If your organization operates with a mind-set that causes you to pass on a top prospect just because he hasn't used the same brand of lab equipment you have while doing similar experiments, then you're wasting your time worrying about getting top talent at all.

DIVERSITY RECRUITING

Diversity is one of the most difficult, and sometimes controversial, aspects of college recruiting. Competition is fierce, and the number of quality minority candidates is disproportionately low. Consider the plight of employers in the technology sector. Of all engineering students across the country, only 6.6 percent are African American, 7 percent are Hispanic, and less than 1 percent are Native American. One recruiting manager from a medium-sized software company said, "It makes me pull my hair out."

We are confident that you can improve your diversity recruiting results by using the strategy and tactics throughout this book, but here are some additional guidelines for approaching this unique front in the war for young talent.

Define the diversity you want

There are many reasons you may want to hire and retain a diverse workforce. Perhaps you want your team to reflect the diversity of your changing customer base. Many consumer products makers, for instance, seek to hire people of certain ethnicities specifically for their insights into the expanding Hispanic market in America. Or maybe you just want to ensure that your employees can offer different perspectives to help you better tackle complex problems.

Whether you want to add diversity along dimensions of ethnicity, gender, or physical challenges, the first step to finding talented people in your target groups is to make your intentions and reasons clear to everyone in your organization.

Use the same hiring process as for any other recruit

Many times a CEO's urgent directive for diversity hiring causes an HR department to get so worked up about getting the diversity hires they want that they abandon their normal recruiting processes in the name of "getting the job done." But problems occur when recruiters overzealously handle the process of identifying, screening, and hiring top diversity prospects without involving the business units those recruits will work for, as they would have done with any other recruit. We've seen cases in which HR doesn't tell a business unit they are getting an intern or an entry-level employee until only a few weeks or days before the recruit arrives.

This causes two kinds of problems. First, the business units do not feel invested in the new hires, and may not be properly prepared or equipped to manage and mentor a new hire. Second, the diversity recruits feel awkward when they talk to other recruits and realize that their hiring process was completely different.

Show some class

Because diversity recruiting is so competitive, many employers unfortunately get desperate and display some very tacky behavior. One well-known company was focused on meeting African American students at the MIT career fair. When a group of white students approached the employer's booth, the recruiter said, "Sorry, we aren't interested in you, but here is a gift, and do you have any black friends? We really need them." Of course, the comment made everyone uncomfortable, including college staff at the fair.

Here's another common act of desperation to avoid. A recruiter for a software company called an academic department's internship program saying he needed to fill 20 jobs with talented minority students from the department. When the recruiter asked the department head for "the list," of course the internship director explained, "We just can't do that."

Commit for the long term

Companies are often bewildered when they get few applications after making an on-campus presentation to a student group of their desired diversity segment. Randy Wilson, who is Director of Diversity Programs at the University of Texas M. D. Anderson Cancer Center in Houston, says the students are a bit skeptical of employers who pay special attention to them because they know that the "over-the-top" interest in them can stop as soon as an offer letter is signed: "In the diversity recruiting arena, companies should be focusing on building a great career path, experience, and in retaining employees. Anyone can do the smoke and mirrors during the recruiting process, and most students will easily see through that."

Whether you drop in once or invest in building long-term relationships with certain groups, the students will notice. As Wilson says, "Minority groups have strong social networks," so be assured that word of your recruiting practices will travel fast and it will stick.

SETTING RECRUITING GOALS

Once you know what kind of people you're looking for, it's time to ask the question "How many?" And the key to good recruiting is to ask "How many?" multiple times.

The single problem that plagues the most recruiters is what we call the conversion complex—the tendency to focus on only one conversion metric, such as InternsToFullTimeEmployees or ApplicantsToHires, and do whatever's easiest to make the number look better on paper, regardless of what's actually best for building a strong talent pipeline. It's usually the fault of the organization as a whole when it does not support the recruiter in sticking to finding the candidates with the firm's most desired attributes, and when it bases the recruiter's entire performance evaluation on just one standard conversion metric.

The conversion complex is what causes the disconnect between what organization leaders say their goals are and how they act in recruiting. One day an executive may say he wants to find, attract, and hire only the best people possible. The next he encourages a frontline recruiter to do whatever it takes to just push more past interns through the recruiting process, perhaps ignoring their past performance. So which is it? Do you want the best people or do you just want people, any people, to stay once they've started?

If you're an executive, ask yourself if you've done this. If you're a recruiter trying to operate within these circumstances (rather than changing jobs), here's how to give yourself the best chance to succeed.

Set as many minigoals as possible leading up to the big goal

You'll never hit your big goal if you just go through the recruiting motions all year, hoping that the numbers work out in the end. Set goals for each stage of the recruiting process, including the following:

Career fair
Information sessions
Applications received
First-round interviews
Second- /final-round interviews
Offers extended
Offers accepted

Don't say, "We're going to try to meet as many students as possible at the career fair." Decide you're going to meet 100 students. Then, instead of leaving pleased that you met "a lot of students" when you met only 59, you'll work hard throughout the day, intermittently gauging and adjusting your pace, to make sure you meet 100 or more.

Don't *hope* you hit your numbers—*know* you will

One evening a recruiter walked into our office at MIT and said, "I have 15 T-shirts I was going to give away at my seminar tonight, but no one came, so would you please give them to some of your students?" She couldn't figure out why no students attended her seminar. After all, she had put an ad in the campus newspaper and flyers on bulletin boards.

If you don't tell students about your events through direct contact (e-mail, phone, or in person) and advertise through very targeted, student-respected channels (student group leaders, career advisors, internship program staff), you'll be left hoping for attendance and wondering why you don't get it, too. But if you do those things, you can get commitments to attend from some students and better estimate how many others will probably show up.

Track the effectiveness of your advertising channels

This can be as easy as adding a question to the sign-in sheet at your information session. Ask: "How did you hear about this event? (Check all that apply.)" Here are the results from a recent event the MIT UPOP program cohosted with an employer:

95%	E-mail from academic administrator
70%	E-mail through a student group or living group
30%	Postcard mailed to me
10%	Ad in the newspaper

Now it's easy to calculate which advertising channels to maintain and which ones are best to cut if the budget is tight in the future.

Consult your campus partners when you don't hit your numbers

One year a Microsoft recruiter called our staff and said, "Our last round of interviews didn't go so well. Only 10 percent reached the second round, and we were hoping for more. Can we show you the interview list and discuss how we could do a better job of reaching the right students?" Excellent. Your campus partners will know the students better than you and will be able to help you spot any circumstances on campus that might be causing your recruiting problems—like a hot company that's presenting new competition or a new academic program that's removing talent from the corporate recruiting pool.

Give your boss a reality check

If you think the numbers you've been asked to hit are ridiculous, counter with some common sense. We've heard goals like "We want to hire 10 economics majors" when there are only 25 students in the department.

If you can't eyeball it, get a second opinion. Some of the best benchmarking data available are published by the National Association of Colleges and Employers (NACE), the Society for Human Resource Management (SHRM), and the Scott Resource Group (led by recruiting expert Mary Scott). These organizations conduct extensive nationwide surveys each year that are cited in the *Wall Street Journal* and other leading business publications. (Note: Even if the goals your boss is setting do seem realistic, it's a good idea to benchmark them against data from these organizations.)

If you're charged with the daunting task of hiring a great full-time employee in your first year on a campus with a competitive recruiting climate, tell the boss to get that expectation out of his mind immediately. It's not impossible, but it is improbable. Tell him we said so, and suggest lowering the bar to hiring an intern for starters.

Question your policies and make sure the rules you set up are driving top talent to your organization

One automaker has a policy of hiring full-time, entry-level employees only from their pool of past interns. The idea may sound good at first, but it poses a serious conflict with getting the best people for the organization. The intern-only rule limits the company's full-time recruiting pool to the few students who happened to have been brought in as underclass students. It prevents the company from getting its share of talent from the largest recruiting pool on campus—seniors. And, unless the company starts hiring many more interns, frontline recruiters will push less-than-excellent intern prospects through the system just to fill open positions.

Until recently, Google had been very strict about hiring only people with stellar grades—almost no B's allowed. Since it's human nature to want to feel like you're better than your subordinates, this policy prevented hiring managers from perpetually lowering recruiting standards and diluting the talent pool.

Google always knew that grades can't tell you everything about a student's potential as an employee, but it was the one clear-cut metric everyone could agree on. Google knew that there were great prospects out there who didn't graduate magna cum laude, but it figured that as long as it kept bringing in enough great people who did post straight A's, it didn't need anyone else. Now, as its recruiting needs have grown even more, Google is easing up on the GPA requirement and placing more importance on a variety other attributes to screen prospects.

Propose metrics that better measure what's really important

Everyone wishes they had better metrics than those silly conversion rates, but rarely do they try anything different. They say it's too

difficult. All of recruiting is difficult, but you can make some amazing improvements if you put in the work. Our best advice: Invent
two or three metrics that make sense—metrics that reflect your
long-term perspective on recruiting rather than a nonrecruiter's
short-term, transactional thinking of last-minute conversions; metrics that measure quality of hires rather than just quantity. Then try
them. Test them. Discuss them. Of course, you can still track the
data to satisfy your conversion complex, but you shouldn't let it define your organization or your goals.

❖ *Chapter Takeaway:* The very first thing you should do when starting, overhauling, or even tweaking a college recruiting program is to
articulate what you are and what you are not, decide which talents
and skills are absolutely most important for you to find in recruiting
prospects, and choose the bars to shoot for in executing your plans.
In each of these exercises, take nothing for granted just because
that's how things have been done in the past. With your experience
and this book at your disposal, you can surely create new practices
that make your recruiting better than ever.

10

Build Your Team and Go

When you want to win more battles in the war for young talent, it's tempting to think, *We just need better recruiters.* No doubt it helps if the individuals in the demanding role of frontline recruiter are supertalented themselves, but you have to build strong teams around them to reach the level of the best recruiting companies like Microsoft and McKinsey. Operating a world-class recruiting machine takes commitment and cooperation from people throughout your organization—the information session presenters in sync with the HR team in sync with the eventual managers and mentors of your new recruits and more—all with the same goals, all with the same strategy, all singing from the same sheet of music. And, not surprisingly, the conductor of that symphony must be at the top.

MAKE SURE YOUR CEO IS RECRUITING TEAM MEMBER NO. 1

As with any other initiative in business, to have people throughout your organization care about recruiting the best, your CEO must first show that he or she cares.

Bob Kraft, a cofounder of Florida-based Power Systems Manu-facturing, which employs over 100 engineers, frequently attends campus career fairs himself or sends another senior leader in his place. "Every engineer who works for us, I've interviewed person-ally," said Kraft, "because making sure we get the right people for the company is one of my most important jobs, if not *the* most im-portant."

In *The War for Talent*, authors Michaels, Handfield-Jones, and Axelrod tell the story of Greg Summe, who led a talent revolution when he became CEO of life sciences technology company EG&G (now PerkinElmer). After the company's stock price tripled in his first three years on the job, Summe attributed it largely to his talent mind-set, saying, "People were my number one issue three years ago. They are my number one issue now. And people will be my number one issue three years from now."

When an organization's leadership thinks like that—*and* makes its view known to everyone—it's much easier to garner enthusiasm and support for effective recruiting. But, most important, it gives em-ployees a new appreciation for the people who do the recruiting, es-pecially when the CEO pitches in on the front lines.

WHAT IT TAKES TO BE A GREAT RECRUITER

The stereotype that being nice is all you need to be a recruiter couldn't be further from the truth. Being congenial and enjoying working with people certainly helps, but it takes much more to be a great recruiter. You have to sell, listen, and improvise with the best of them. You have to be a strategic marketer and a master relation-ship builder, with the polish of a politician.

Think it's hard to sell a widget? Try selling a 40-plus-hour/week experience to a college student worried about choosing the wrong job in the biggest decision of his life. You've got to display the patience of a kindergarten teacher, wield the sage advice of a career counselor, and convey the compassion of a parent—and do it all while having to mobilize a large team and operate on less money than you really need.

Recruiting demands a complicated skill set and entails a mixed bag of responsibilities that few people possess. Smart recruiting companies, like Microsoft and McKinsey, view recruiting as a bona fide business expertise—alongside sales, marketing, operations, and the like. In fact, many of the best recruiters *are* the best because they have previously worked and succeeded in other capacities like sales, marketing, operations, and more. That's the thing to remember: Great recruiters can do anything, so you had better be as committed to keeping them on your team as you are to retaining new college graduates.

HOW DO YOUR RECRUITERS MEASURE UP?

Students intuitively rate recruiters on three factors. We call them the three C's. Not *calm*, *cool*, and *collected*, although those do help, but *confidence*, *competence*, and *control*—what students look for and talk to their friends about. The more support your entire organization gives its recruiters, the higher your recruiters' 3C scores will be.

Confidence

The self-confidence of recruiters is largely determined by how your organization views them. Ask yourself:

How important are the people who are finding our next generation of leaders?

Do we treat the recruiting function as a cost center or a place that adds tremendous value?

If "contact is king," shouldn't the people making the contact be respected as royalty in the organization?

Your answers to these questions have a large effect on how your recruiters operate, how your other employees interact with them during campus visits, and, ultimately, how they are perceived by students. If inside your organization a recruiter is seen as merely a glorified secretary, chances are that college students will view the recruiter the same way.

Competence

Your campus recruiters must have good answers about what your company does, what your industry is all about, what's happening now to your business, the history of your organization, potential career paths, what your alumni are doing now, and more. If they don't, students will think, *Well, this person is just from HR*, dismiss their worth, and try to get to other people in the company. An uninformed recruiter not only hurts your reputation on campus, but his inability to answer questions creates more work for the other people on your team.

Control

Microsoft recruiters are always equipped to ask some technical questions in addition to the standard behavioral interview, and the recruiter's opinions weigh heavily in Microsoft's hiring decisions.

It's fine if your behind-the-scenes HR people don't have power in a recruiting decision, but it must be clear to students that recruiters on campus who take prospects to lunch or conduct interviews actually have some control over their fate.

FOUR WAYS TO RECRUIT MORE RECRUITERS

Students are wise to tricks like the old sorority ploy of putting a carefully selected group of the prettiest, most articulate girls in the "rush" room and hiding everyone else, banking on prospects never discovering that the entire organization isn't full of aspiring Miss America contestants.

Your target recruits are smart. (That's why you want them, after all.) They'll quickly see through any plan to expose them to only your five best people and, afterward, won't trust you as far as they can throw you.

Our best advice: The bigger your recruiting team, the better. The more people actively looking out for prospects, the easier identifying top talent will be. The more people trained in the art of appealing to what college students want for their first jobs, the less likely a prospect will deem someone incompetent and be turned off by your organization. And the more people period, the easier it is to produce great events that help you attract and evaluate target recruits. Here are four ways to recruit more recruiters to get those benefits:

Spend as much time thinking about your recruiters as your recruits

When you're trying so hard to find great talent for all parts of your organization, it's easy to overlook the need for people with great talent for finding that talent. Keep your eye out for recruiter prospects constantly, but establish a monthly or quarterly habit of reviewing new contacts inside and outside your organization and evaluate their potential to help you recruit.

Ask for referrals

If you work in a big organization, you can't possibly know all the people with natural talent for recruiting, and if you work in a small company, you may not have seen something in someone that others have. So ask managers and department heads to recommend people you should consider involving in recruiting.

Track your new hires

Evaluate your new hires for recruiting potential as they come on board and plant seeds in their minds early on. Using your personal relationships with these entry-level employees can yield participation driven by their personal desire, which is especially helpful when their managers are reluctant to approve time away from their core job functions to assist with recruiting the next class of college graduates.

Make recruiting an opportunity they can't refuse

If it's clear that recruiting can push their own careers forward, employees from all over the organization will be eager to join in. Develop training workshops to teach these recruiting helpers how to aid your success on campus, and demonstrate how recruiting skills transfer to other aspects of their careers, such as making persuasive presentations, closing business deals, and growing their networks in their everyday jobs. Make it known that campus recruiting provides opportunities to have fun traveling with colleagues on the company dime and you should have no problem growing your team.

SYNCHRONIZE HR AND YOUR EXTENDED RECRUITING TEAM

In the race for today's top young talent, one global communications company can't seem to get its recruiting efforts out of the gate because of a lack of coordination between HR and other business units. The HR department is centralized and thinks that if it can just fill a certain number of spots, the job is done. But the business units, the organizations actually hosting summer interns and taking on entry-level hires, have other ideas. They want a certain type of student for their groups, or they want no one at all. The result: recruiting so ineffective that the HR staff has to apologize to top universities for not being able to attract and hire their students.

In this scenario, there's an obvious mismatch of goals and expectations between HR and other business units, one that can be solved only by open discussion among all parties and a final directive from senior leadership that all parties buy into. It's a difficult situation, but it can be fixed, as can all of the rifts between HR and other business units. Here are five tips for getting everyone on the same team:

Buck the budget cycle

Many HR teams know they should always be recruiting if they want to find the best people for their organizations, but they don't want to waste their time when business units have yet to say how many new hires they want. The business units say it's the budget cycle that's to blame for not knowing until March or April how many interns and new hires they can afford. That's baloney. When it comes to the acquisition of your most valuable assets (talented people), you need to do whatever fancy forecasting it takes. Don't let a spreadsheet steal control of your organization from your people. Figure out how to get your college recruiting team its talent requisition numbers by September or October. Make the numbers conservative if you have to, but give your recruiters a directive to hire. Recruiters who show up on campus "just in case" give off a bad vibe that turns off students.

Deliver consequences for noncooperation

Managers often look forward to a day away from the office or a trip back to their alma maters to help with recruiting. But beware of dilettante recruiters! Anyone who consistently doesn't get you the information you need or doesn't stay on the recruiting message you've worked so hard to create should not participate in your recruiting.

Period. IBM, in its much-improved college recruiting of late, has gotten great results with this practice. Individuals who don't share the recruiting load are off the IBM recruiting team. One college recruiter said, "If they don't get it, they're gone. It's a difficult conversation to have with people, but you've gotta do it." If business-unit managers really want young talent, they'll learn their lesson and change their ways.

Recruiters, show what you know!

Although we believe strong measures are sometimes required to get business units in gear, recruiters are sometimes too quick to blame low application numbers on a hiring manager who "doesn't know how to write a good job description." If you're the organization's expert on the mind-set of college students because you spend the most time on campus, make it your responsibility to educate everyone else. You should be the final editor of any advertising copy meant for student consumption, and the best way to decrease the amount of reworking required is to help others gain a better understanding of the nuances of attracting young talent. (Hint: Maybe they need to read this book!)

Ensure both parties get to make their contributions

The split interviewing method—in which HR tests for fit and hiring managers test for skills—is great for exactly this reason. But be careful to execute interviews properly to ensure that no one's toes get stepped on. The employers who try to save time by doing one interview, with both the HR representative and the hiring manager in the same room, only encourage conflict. Inevitably, the hiring manager wins because her decision is traditionally the final one in the hiring process. Keep the interviews separate. The hiring manager's decision should simply be the last decision in recruiting, not the most important one, especially after the long process of identifying, attracting, and evaluating talent—an endeavor that takes a lot of work.

Conduct formal recruiting training

We've mentioned several times the importance of training your people to give great answers to questions from prospects and to get the most out of interviews. The most valuable reason for conducting formal recruiting training, however, is to bring your extended recruiting team together. While you can handpick your core recruiting team and the employees who help deliver company presentations on campus, the business-unit hiring managers and the direct managers of your future recruits are outside your control. Administering a formal recruiting training program is your strongest weapon to combat the attitude that "anyone can do recruiting." The time spent working together to achieve a common goal is the best thing you can do to strengthen your extended recruiting team before you get to campus.

✤ *Chapter Takeaway:* To make your recruiting machine run smoothly, the importance of both the act of recruiting and the people doing the recruiting must be declared by the top management of the organization and appreciated throughout the organization. To make your machine run robustly, you must get people throughout the firm to join your extended recruiting team and do whatever it takes to get your business units and HR working together.

· PART FOUR ·

FREE CONSULTING

———

Here are nine frequently asked questions, along with our best advice for how to handle the tough college recruiting situations your organization is bound to face.

Q: We are having great success recruiting interns from our reach universities, but we can't seem to sign anyone for full-time positions. What should we do?

The problem could be in either your internship program or your full-time recruiting program.

The key to finding what's broken in both cases is getting honest, even brutally honest, feedback. Remember the recruiter in Chapter 8 who got all the dirt on what her interns really thought of their summer experience? She solicited regular input from the interns' managers, she asked other interns about what they said candidly while on the job, and she delayed asking the tough questions of her target recruits until they were far enough removed from the job to not be guarded with their answers. You may have to do that and more to gather the intelligence you need to turn your interns into employees.

You'll discover problems that you have the power to change, such as your compensation package is a bit lower than your competition's, or a few managers in your organization dropped the ball when it came to mentoring the interns.

Overcoming other problems will require more work and tougher decisions. Sometimes the nature of a business makes it impossible to offer interns challenging work in only 10 to 12 weeks because it takes longer to train people on the necessary equipment. If this is true in your organization, we suggest recruiting fewer interns from your reach schools so you can focus more on delivering an amazing experience to them, or recruiting no interns from those schools at all. This may seem crazy, but it's even crazier to continue past actions that haven't produced the results you want.

Whenever you recruit interns and don't deliver an amazing experience, you do more harm than good. One important reason for recruiting interns is to enhance your image on campus, but giving student interns something bad to say about your company is worse than having no intern experience at all for anyone to talk about. (See Chapter 3 if you need a refresher.)

It is possible to make great full-time hires without having an internship program at all. If your competitors hire interns just because they think they have to run an internship program, and they don't deliver a great experience in those 10 to 12 weeks, their interns and other prospects will associate negative connotations with their names. If you elect to not host interns and reallocate the money and time you would have used for intern recruiting to bolster your full-time recruiting efforts, you can sell them on joining you without having to fight negative buzz on campus.

Also, remember that accepting a full-time job is the biggest decision of a college student's life. If you are aware of sticking points in your program from past recruits, you must address them directly and as frequently as possible on campus. For example, if past interns have said that your location is boring but you now support a social club to help new hires find housing in your town's best neighborhood for young people, acknowledge the past problem and explain what you're doing to fix it when you speak to students on campus. Your honesty and effort to make new hires' lives better will make them feel special, which is key to signing full-timers.

Q: We don't have many alumni from the schools where we want to start recruiting. How can we conquer those campuses?

Your target recruits want to feel like you understand where they're coming from. Alumni from recruits' schools, of course, automatically get the benefit of the doubt. But you can earn much of the same credibility if you follow the recommendations in Chapter 4 for transforming yourself into an honorary alum: Take the campus tour, get to know as many people who study and work at the school, and read the campus newspaper.

Recruits like to know that your organization was a good choice for their predecessors. To give recruits this peace of mind, you can leverage alumni from peer schools as well. Peer schools are usually the colleges the recruits applied to in addition to the one they attend. If you are recruiting at Georgia Tech but don't have employees who studied there, make sure to talk up and introduce your staff from other respected engineering schools like Purdue, Carnegie Mellon, or MIT.

Hiring alumni from any elite school helps you recruit. Period. In the minds of college students, companies that employ alumni from elite schools do have a certain cachet, so flaunt what you've got. It's a huge advantage to have students thinking, *If she went to that company after going to Duke, it must be good.*

Finally, having all the alumni or all the Harvard grads in the world won't make a lick of difference if you don't spend time on campus getting to know students personally and establishing real connections with staff and faculty. There's no substitute for personal contact, and you actually need more of it to make up for not already having the network enjoyed by alumni.

Q: We're pretty successful at identifying, attracting, and signing the interns and full-time hires we want. But we typically lose a lot of those new hires after about two years. What can we do?

Two years seems to be the magic number in the minds of most talented college graduates. It's as if their brains are hardwired to think they have to try something new around that time. If you try to fight it, you'll lose. But if you use this information to anticipate and plan for the two-year itch, you'll have a fighting chance of keeping entry-level hires longer.

To sign with your organization right out of college, recruits have to believe that you'll provide them the best opportunity to advance their career at *that* point. And, to stay with your organization beyond two years, they have to believe that you'll provide the best opportunity to advance their career at *that* point, too.

When Tom Cruise, as sports agent Jerry Maguire in the movie of that name, asks his professional football playing client, played by Cuba Gooding Jr., what it will take to maintain their working relationship, Gooding's answer is simple: "Show me the money!" Staying with your organization may not be all about the "kwan"—as they say in the movie—but your top talent will at least be thinking, *Show me the opportunity!* Maybe that golden opportunity is the chance to start managing projects and people or the option to move to a new division. One best practice is to structure a three- or four-year program that calls for switching to a new position or taking an assignment in a foreign country after the second year.

Many new hires want to eventually attend graduate school. If you have the resources, consider supporting them through a part-time program while working in exchange for their commitment to a certain number of years afterward. But beware that top performers still want assurance that they will be promoted to a new role within a reasonable amount of time after completing graduate school. What's the point of earning a graduate degree if it won't advance your career? If new hires think the reward for a graduate degree is just more of the same in your organization, they'll pass on the offer to keep working for you after a couple of years. But if you have a culture that not only encourages internal transfers but actually executes them, you'll have much more success retaining top young talent.

Q: We performed a rigorous self-assessment like you described in Chapter 9: "Define Yourself and Your Goals," and we honestly didn't find anything that makes our organization truly special. What can we do?

Every organization is special in some way. When students complain that a company seems generic, the truth is it's the company recruiting materials or the company's presentation on campus that seems generic. A bit of research on your part—drawing from prior knowledge or asking friends within the organization or even valued clients what they admire—usually turns up something about the company that surprises or excites the students.

The more you can get inside the minds of your target recruits, the easier it will be for you to see what about your organization, or even a specific team, would seem special to them. Or, you may discover a piece of low-hanging fruit—that is, an existing program you can add to or otherwise ramp up to make your organization more of a standout in the minds of recruits from now on.

Still, many organizations, especially really big ones, have a problem with this. They claim they're too big to undergo changes that actually sweep through all parts of the company. In this case, the key is to start with one small group at a time.

Let's say you have a group of 20 employees in the marketing department who are willing to commit resources and energy to transforming their small part of the organization. The managers of the group are on board and want this change to happen. Perhaps HR can support them in establishing a rotation program within their group for new hires, create formal training classes to expose recruits to many parts of the industry, and even support social events to mold the group into a community. A group like that would be something really special, and as beneficial for your organization's performance as it would be for campus recruiting.

If even one group is this remarkable and you make it clear that you're looking for special people for this specific group, recruits will respond.

Yes, starting a pilot program will probably receive some internal pushback, but getting great people is worth the struggle. And when the program works, you'll be the hero who gets to expand it throughout the company.

Q: Our organization is widely known for one function, but it's critical to our success to recruit top talent for other departments that might be considered back-office or noncore parts of our business. How can we get great people for those departments when we're competing with organizations who are known primarily for those functions?

For the sake of this question, let's assume you're a financial services firm. When students hear your brand name on campus, they envision trading floors. But you also need state-of-the-art technology systems, which means you need some of the absolute best technical minds on your team. How can you get those recruits when companies like Microsoft, Google, and Apple are known as the big guys in technology?

It's tough. Recruiting the best for noncore functional groups might be the greatest challenge of all. Not only are you competing with Microsoft and Google, but you are also competing with your own firm, because what students perceive to be "your firm" is actually another department.

As we describe in Chapter 9, the first thing to do is to define yourself not in the context of your organization as a whole but specifically as your department: Your department offers the unique opportunity to apply technical skills to financial problems.

Because technology isn't your *real* business, the next barrier to overcome is students' perceptions that the problems you address are not as hard core as the technology challenges taken on at Microsoft and Google. To counter this thinking and change students' minds, you need direct access to and personal interaction with potential recruits.

To prove that the work your group does is as challenging and interesting as it gets, partner with a faculty member who teaches a technology class to base a class project on a problem that your team has solved in the past. (It's okay to tweak elements of the project to protect your proprietary information.) You can also sponsor a competition on campus to show that problems in your industry are just as challenging as the ones technology companies deal with.

Beyond changing students' minds about the work you do, you have to prove that a three- to five-year stint in your department will do wonders for their careers whether they stay with you or move on. Students worry about a company's back-office functions becoming dead-end positions. They worry that, should they want to leave technology, an investment bank's technology group won't be perceived as a stepping stone to a job at Google or admission to business school.

Have students talk to alumni who worked for you and then made a successful move to a technology company or a top-tier business school. If you've had employees leave to start their own consulting firms specializing in helping financial companies with technology, let your potential recruits know. Share evidence of great career paths within your department. You may have senior managers or vice presidents who started in the analyst program. Celebrate those employees and make sure your recruits understand how great those jobs are. Let recruits know that those people are compensated very well and that they are truly leaders in the company.

It's important to give young hires as much evidence as possible that working for you will be a great stepping stone to whatever they might want to do in the future.

Let them know that back-office employees are not treated like second-class citizens. This is by far the hardest thing to prove. If your front-office people really do treat the back-office people poorly and don't give them professional respect, it will be as hard to recruit great new talent as it is for you to stay there yourself.

Q: A student we've identified as one of our top prospects for next year's entry-level positions turned us down for an internship this summer to work with a competing firm. We are certain our competitor will give her an offer at the end of this summer to join them full-time when she graduates in another year. What can we do to stay in the game?

Your competitor has a clear advantage because day in and day out during the internship they have the chance to sell the recruit on returning to work for them. But notice we said *chance*. There is a possibility your competitor will squander the opportunity to make the full-time hire. Here's how you might put yourself in position to capitalize on a competitor's mistakes.

Again, contact is king. If you lose touch, you will lose recruits. Don't be overbearing, though. Just make enough contact so she doesn't forget about you.

If you are in the same location as your competitor, set up a summer evening event (or several) for your top prospects, whether they're interning with you or not. Let prospects know the event is invitation-only and plan it to coincide with something exciting like a company-sponsored appearance of a big-name guest speaker or the unveiling of a new product. This not only shows prospects that you are very interested in them, but also that your organization does some really cool stuff. The same rules apply here as during the academic year: Make sure your prospects get to meet and chat with as many interesting people from your team as possible.

If you are not in the same location as your competitor, stay in contact with your prospect by phone and e-mail. When possible, perhaps in conjunction with a regularly (or creatively) scheduled business trip, have one of your recruiting team members visit the prospect in person. The more direct contact, the better.

Talking about interviews is another way to keep your company top of mind. Before she goes to your competing firm for the summer, let her know you are so excited about her potential that you are going to advance her to the final round of interviews in your full-time recruiting process next fall. This not only tells her she's getting a guaranteed interview, but also that she is just one step away from a full-time offer.

Planting that seed is your best bet for preventing a prospect from accepting your competitor's full-time offer at the end of the summer without at least interviewing with you first. Many students accept end-of-summer offers just because they are a sure thing, and students don't yet know how many interviews and offers they will get once the fall recruiting season begins. To counter this acceptance-by-uncertainty of prospects interning at competing firms, some investment banks actually start doing first-round interviews in the summer so they don't miss out on recruits just because of timing. If you're not organized to start that early, your promise of a final-round interview during the normal recruiting season should still give your prospects enough confidence to not take the first offer they receive at the end of the summer.

Caution: If a prospect accepts an internship with a competitor, *do not* give her a full-time offer in desperation, before or during the summer. You need to maintain the impression that your process is competitive and rigorous, even if you already know you want to hire her. If you give her an offer prematurely, she will seek out every company she is interested in and use your offer as a bargaining chip to expedite their process for her. In fact, you'll be the only employer with which she draws out the process. Even if after searching high and low she doesn't get a job she likes better, your offer won't seem very appealing because it will just be what's left over. You don't want any recruit starting work with that attitude.

Q: We usually allow recruits one month to accept or reject our job offers, but more and more recruits are asking for extensions or rejecting us after 30 days because they're still hoping to receive better offers from other employers. How can we close more deals within the one-month window?

First, you may not be starting your process at the right time. There can be an advantage to making offers before your competitors, but don't do it too far in advance. This is especially important for employers who are new to a school and don't yet have a strong reputation on campus. If you're relatively unknown on campus and your offer expires before the other employers your prospect wants to apply to, the prospect will most likely decline your offer in favor of waiting for potential interviews and offers with the other employers. In this case, a little competition is good because, even if you're making the best offer in the world, there's no way students will believe that if they have nothing with which to compare it.

Second, if students are rejecting you even when they don't have other offers in hand, you need to find out what the problem is fast. It's not a good sign if, by the time companies start making offers, you don't have good enough relationships with the candidates themselves to figure out what is wrong, but that's water under the bridge. Call every one of your superconnectors on campus if that's what it takes, but find out what's up immediately.

In Chapter 6 we explained how you can offer incentives like signing bonuses and choice of location/manager/group to encourage students to decide by a certain date—obviously, the earlier, the better. Sometimes these incentives won't be enough, and you'll have to compromise your deadlines. If a student is waiting for another employer to make a decision, say that you are willing to grant an extension if the other company will expedite their process also. This way you're not bearing the burden by yourself. Most students will respect your firmness if you are also kind and reasonable.

When necessary, ask the prospect directly, "What would we have to do to get you to accept this offer now?" If the student's wish is one you can grant, great. If it's unreasonable or impossible, that's unfortunate, but at least you learn that it's not going to work before delaying further. Then you can immediately proceed to your next best prospect.

Q: What can I do if my company currently has a terrible reputation in the marketplace because of some recent bad news (e.g., going in and out of bankruptcy, involvement in a scandal, or laying off employees)?

Your target recruits certainly don't want to read bad news about you in the *Wall Street Journal*, but there is usually an opportunity to turn lemons into lemonade here. If the scandal is really over or the layoffs have actually stopped, you may be able to sell students on the chance to rebuild your organization from the ground up. Perhaps new hires will have more responsibility than they would have had in your organization's previous state, and maybe there are more opportunities for advancement now that your firm is in flux.

Still, a recent downturn, scandal, or bad press is not an easy sell. You have to prove that your reputation won't hurt a student's chances of switching industries or being admitted to graduate school in a few years. You also need to show evidence of positive progress your organization has made and get other people on campus to back up your story. It's more important than ever to have direct personal contact with students, because students will be much more likely to trust an individual they know than the battered brand of a company itself.

If your crisis is still going while you are recruiting on campus, attracting top talent is far more difficult. Your best bet is to recruit for one special group (a strategy we described earlier in this chapter) and to do your best to show students that this particular group is completely separate from the organization's problems.

Q: We are a small, young company with a great culture and an exciting product. How can we compete with big companies who have deep pockets for recruiting?

Start-ups actually have several inherent competitive advantages over big companies when it comes to recruiting new college graduates. In a young company, everyone is expected to contribute to almost every function, which is ideal for a young recruit whose primary goal is to be exposed to as many new work experiences as possible. You're short on resources, so nearly every piece of every project is mission-critical, which makes a young recruit feel important and highly valuable. Your small size naturally lends itself to having a tight-knit community, which college students are used to. And, of course, there is that chance that your organization could really take off. College students know that the next Google will turn more entry-level workers into millionaires than Procter & Gamble will.

Where you might struggle is in allaying their fears of being able to leverage their time with you to get into grad school or even to switch to a bigger company. Use the suggestions we've offered throughout the book to make sure they know that working with you will expand their options, not limit them.

As for your exciting product and great culture, you'll have to do more show-and-tell than a big company that's already famous for those things. Do as many product demonstrations on campus as you can, and arrange visits to your company. If you have relationships with professors in fields related to your core work, offer to sponsor a class field trip and tailor the tour to the professor's needs also.

Consider partnering with other small companies. If you join together with a few other start-ups or established small firms (and student groups, of course) to run an event about what it's like to work for companies like yours, you'll draw much more of a crowd than if you go it alone because no one knows your name.

Another key is targeting the right students. First, look for the students involved in entrepreneurship clubs or business plan competitions. These students have already identified themselves as interested in working in a start-up environment. Of course, they'd love to found their own companies, but most college students simply don't have the resources or experience to do that, regardless of their desire. Sell them on the idea of learning from the inside of a start-up to prepare for running their own company someday.

We also recommend that young and small companies begin targeting prospects as early as their freshman or sophomore year. Most established companies don't want to recruit these students because they are so focused on converting junior interns to senior full-time hires. As a result, the younger students on college campuses are desperate for opportunities to learn about new industries and career opportunities and to prove their worth and build up experience, so they'll be open to any company willing to hire them for internships.

Make a big deal out of your hiring young interns. Use all the channels mentioned in Chapters 4 and 5 (e.g., internship programs, class mailing lists, student groups, classes that are mostly for underclass students), and you will draw a lot of first- and second-year students, which provides you a huge, impressionable audience to share your story with. Furthermore, you'll attract even more students if you're offering advice that they can act on to advance their careers, even if they don't get one of your internships.

Explain to prospects that for this summer you can hire only a limited number of students (perhaps one to three) but that you're there to recruit for the long term. Just because they don't get an offer doesn't mean you are not interested. Use your informal conversations and formal interviews not only to find a few students to track all the way through college, but to build a large pipeline of prospects to stay in touch with for the future. If you do all this and deliver on your promises of a great work experience, the summer stories that the few interns you do hire tell their friends will have a good chance of spreading to half the student body. You'll go from a complete no-body to the worst-kept secret on campus, and your recruiting in sub-sequent years will become easier and easier.

THERE IS NO end to the interesting and challenging situations that arise from recruiting top young talent, but we hope this gets you well on your way to tackling some of the most important ones. We are confident that by adding the principles and tactics in this book to your own experience and creativity in the field, you can succeed in a competitive recruiting battle on any college campus.

To read more free consulting, ask a question, or share a story of how you've used something in this book for a recruiting win, please visit www.AlwaysRecruiting.com. There you can also learn how to engage us in paid consulting to help define your recruiting strategy and tune up all parts of your recruiting machine.

APPENDIX

We discuss job postings on page 128. The first two samples that follow show more specifically the kinds of mistakes recruiters make in job postings, along with suggestions for how to address those mistakes. The Before Critique highlights mistakes, the Analysis gives our overall impression, and the After Critique is the *Recruit or Die* makeover. We also include a job posting we like, courtesy of the Peace Corps, as well as a sample "feel good" ad that's all the rage right now; it may be effective for big-brand companies but may not work so well for others. This appendix should give you all the tools you need to create job postings that get results.

Job Posting No. 1: Before Critique

Note: Authors' comments are in script.

ROMNISYS [COMPANY NAME]

Entry-Level Marketing Associate

> *Nobody wants their title to have "entry-level" in it—*
> *not even entry-level candidates.*

Romnisys is a consumer electronics company based in San Francisco. We specialize in cellular products for phones, GPS, and handheld music devices.

> *The first few sentences are your opportunity to excite*
> *candidates about working for you. You can do better*
> *than this.*

The marketing associate is responsible for developing and managing the execution of a broad spectrum of consumer-facing projects, as well as providing business analysis and recommendations in support of a product or multiple products.

> *Broad business terms are too high-level for college*
> *applicants. Be specific and include what the work will*
> *be, what the results will be for their careers, and why*
> *they are meaningful.*

The primary focus will be on our new consumer electronics products.

Principal responsibilities include competitive analysis, pricing, and product marketing. The research aspect involves the following:

- Analyze brand landscape and perform competitive analyses on pricing, cost, and product-materials sourcing.

Too many buzzwords. Try telling a story about what this means. Include specific actions.

- Present best practices on product marketing to various consumer verticals.
- Use existing knowledge of consumer Internet applications to recommend.
- Work with cross-functional teams to create product marketing strategy, supporting the director of marketing and other team members.
- Post–product launch, help develop, implement, and manage plans to build volume and profit.
- Update ARMs for growth planning.

A common mistake is to include internal acronyms.

- Work with team members to create tracking mechanism for products sold. Coordinate with senior management to provide an executive dashboard at weekly briefings.

You will also be responsible for promotions planning, including our annual June gala in Las Vegas.

This is a perfect place to talk about exactly what this project will involve: Las Vegas! That already sounds exciting. Now include specific responsibilities and outcomes.

QUALIFICATIONS:

BA with strong quantitative/analytical curriculum (e.g., finance, marketing, accounting, statistics). One to two years relevant experience with a background in consumer electronics marketing, sales, distribution, or operations desirable.

This sounds like every other company's job posting. Use your qualifications section to differentiate yourself from other organizations.

Analytical experience preferred. Experience with PowerPoint, Excel. Ability to work well with a wide variety of functional disciplines in distributed team environments.

BENEFITS:

Full benefits package including medical, dental, vision, 401(k). Tuition assistance (if applicable). Career mentorship plan.

Fairly standard except for the "career mentorship plan." That sounds interesting—but what does it mean?

SALARY:

Competitive.

DEADLINE:

December 3. Applications should be sent through your school's recruiting Web site. Interviews will be extended by December 10.

Always opt for more contact from your recruits, not less. Unless you're getting thousands of applications, it's also good to give them a single person—with a phone number and e-mail address—to contact with questions.

ANALYSIS

This bland job posting could belong to any consumer company in the world. Beyond using internal acronyms that candidates won't understand, it's just adequate—adequate at explaining which candidates the company is looking for, adequate at explaining the competition, and adequate at explaining job responsibilities.

Unfortunately, adequate doesn't attract extraordinary candidates. Don't make the same mistake this job posting does by using the wrong levels of description. For example, it sometimes describes the job too broadly, using phrases like "develop, implement, and manage plans." College students don't know what that means. They want to know what they will actually be doing. At other times, the job description is too detailed, covering responsibilities like "update ARMs" (what's that?).

The single goal of a job posting is to get qualified applicants to submit an application. We've rewritten it to show you how to be more exciting and attractive to job seekers.

Job Posting No. 1: After Critique

ROMNISYS

Consumer Marketing Associate

Romnisys is a consumer electronics company based in San Francisco, CA, with offices in New York and London. This year, we built the world's first cellular phone with GPS tracking (you may have seen it in the *New York Times*, *Wired* magazine, or online). That was only the first step.

Use your first few sentences to engage recruits and explain why they should care about your organization.

Later this year, we'll release two more products that the world has never seen, and we're looking for a top-caliber consumer marketing associate to help us with marketing strategy and execution. If you use YouTube, instant messaging, and Facebook—and you're interested in taking your online experiences to help shape the marketing of new consumer products—we'd love to talk to you.

What college student wouldn't want to read on to the next paragraph? By explaining the job to them on their terms, you can widen your recruiting net.

OVERVIEW OF POSITION:

We're looking for someone special who understands that marketing and data analysis go hand in hand. Don't worry if you don't already know specific statistical packages; we're more interested in meeting candidates who understand how to think through a problem and analyze the main issues.

As a marketing associate, you will work directly with the director of marketing to understand how our emerging products fit with our consumers' needs.

To your prospects, knowing with whom they'll work is as important as knowing what they'll do.

This involves researching and analyzing the consumer electronics space. Then, you'll help design a strategy to respond to those needs. Finally, you'll implement this strategy, giving you a true end-to-end perspective of product marketing. The combination of creative marketing and analytics will give you a powerful leg up in your long-term career.

High-level description of what they'll be doing and why the work is meaningful for their personal careers.

The marketing associate role is a two-year program, after which candidates have advanced to senior positions within the marketing department, rotated to other departments, joined graduate programs, or continued successful careers at other companies. Some of our past employees have decided to go to graduate school and return to Romnisys in a more advanced position, which we funded through our tuition-assistance program.

Reassures prospects that this job will be a great stepping-stone, not a dead end. And with great benefits like tuition assistance — if you've got it, flaunt it!

THE WORK:

There are three major categories to the marketing associate role, all of which contribute to giving you a detailed, well-rounded experience: competitive intelligence, growth planning, and promotions planning and execution.

Competitive intelligence

We want to know how our product fits into the market, and what other companies are doing. This will take investigation and initiative on your part. We'll ask the general questions and leave it up to you to find the answers.

- How are consumers using our products and competitor products? You'll investigate consumption trends and new uses for our products.

- Is our market growing? Explore trends caused by factors such as season and geography.
- What do the numbers say? Conduct in-depth analyses on promotions and pricing.

Uses an easy-to-understand Q&A format to explain the business tasks. Remember, for most college students, this will be their first full-time job.

Growth planning

How do we plan for growth using imperfect information? As a marketing associate, you will help develop and manage plans to build volume and profit. In other words, you'll help drive our product marketing strategy as we go forward.

Promotions planning and execution

You'll work with senior management to plan and implement promotions for our consumers. For example, in June we host a major marketing event in Las Vegas, which you will be responsible for.

- Coordinate with multiple teams and senior managers to execute annual promotions.
- Manage associated spending budgets.

While working with the director of marketing for these tasks, you'll also be working with cross-functional teams to expose you to other parts of the business.

THE BENEFITS:

We offer all the basics you'd expect: a competitive salary, a comprehensive benefits package (medical, dental, vision), and a 401(k) and pension plan.

You should always cover the basics, even if they're industry standards. Put yourself in the shoes of your recruit, some of whom will have parents asking, "Does the company have health insurance and a 401(k)?"

But the really exciting benefits are in the work itself. By joining us as a marketing associate, you'll be exposed to senior management from day one. We value your goals and your career, so we'll connect you with mentors who can offer you as much guidance as you need. We'll also give you the opportunity to grow by giving you more responsibility within the firm. Here are some of the unusual benefits for our new associates:

- *Mentorship from senior management.* Each marketing associate receives three mentors at all levels of the firm, including senior management.
- *A clear career path.* We want you to be successful, not only in this position, but in your long-term career. To that end, we offer many opportunities after a two-year role as a marketing associate. We'll expose you to other teams within Romnisys to help you find the best fit. If you're interested in graduate school, please ask about our tuition assistance program, which has helped many associates earn a graduate degree and return to Romnisys in a more advanced position.

It's not just about your organization, but your recruits' career. Once you acknowledge that your recruits probably won't retire at your organization, you can start crafting a strategy and message to help them achieve their own goals—and you'll benefit by being on their path.

How to apply:

The application deadline is December 3. You can submit it through your school's jobs Web site or by e-mail (see below). To fill out an application, you'll need to include your résumé, GPA, and a few references. If we see a good fit, we'll call you for a phone interview, after which we may invite you to join us for an in-person interview in our San Francisco or New York office. Don't worry—we'll cover all the expenses, and we'll look forward to learning more about your passions and experience.

> *This job description takes a casual approach to explaining the details of the interview process, putting the applicants at ease. Tailor the logistics of submitting applications to what works for you.*

To learn more about our marketing associate position—including case studies on previous marketing associates, interview tips, and the application itself—visit our consumer marketing associate page at www.romnisys.com/jobs/consumer-marketing-associate.

> *Romnisys includes a link to its Web site, which has more links, videos, Q&A, and more. If your job description has excited recruits, count on them visiting here.*

If you have questions, we're here to answer them. E-mail Jason Michaels, director of recruiting, at jason@romnisys.com or call him at (415) 555-5555.

> *A single point of contact for further questions.*

Job Posting No. 2: Before Critique

THE WORLD HELPER INSTITUTE

Summer Intern

Areas of focus: Global warming, ecological preserves.
Compensation: Small stipend available.
Date of internship: June 30–September 1.

This job description starts out with the bare-bones details, not the best tactic for a nonprofit organization offering very little compensation.

DESCRIPTION:

The intern will assist in various logistical and programming tasks. Tasks include use of Excel, PowerPoint, and Microsoft Word to support policy analysts, such as grant writing, writing materials for our Web site, and designing brochures. Interns may work with our executive director to craft media messages. Graduate students or advanced undergraduate students welcome.

After reading this job description, would you know what the job actually entails? Top candidates will want to know exactly this — and how it helps them.

REQUIREMENTS:

- Attention to detail
- Knowledge of Microsoft Excel, PowerPoint, and Word
- Ability to meet deadlines
- Writing experience (writing experience on the Web desired)
- Some background in marketing and design

- Web design or Web maintenance a plus
- Teamwork experience

Generic description could apply to anyone. The lack of focus will deter top candidates.

DETAILS:

The internship is for 35–40 hours per week, with the option for a full-time position at the conclusion of undergraduate or graduate studies. The position is in downtown Washington, D.C. Application deadline is March 1.

ANALYSIS

This job description is similar to many nonprofit job descriptions we found in our research. Although clearly laid out, this description will fail to excite or inspire applicants, especially the extraordinary ones the World Helper Institute wants to reach. In general, nonprofits have a different recruiting message from for-profit companies: Rather than competing on perks, benefits, and advancement, successful nonprofit recruiters will use the significance of their cause as their primary message. For example, instead of focusing on the technical elements of the job—what software will be used, whom the intern will work with—the World Helper Institute should write about why the work is *meaningful*. Here we rewrite the job posting to better appeal to their target candidates.

Job Posting No. 2: After Critique

THE WORLD HELPER INSTITUTE

Summer Policy Intern

Have you ever cringed when you heard about a local park being leveled for a new shopping mall? Do you have debates with your friends about global warming? Have you been looking for a way to influence public policy to focus on the environment?

Nonprofits and other mission-based organizations should focus on the mission before the logistics of the position.

If this sounds like you, and you're an undergraduate or graduate student, we'd be thrilled to talk to you about an internship opportunity we have beginning this June.

The World Helper Institute is a nonprofit agency founded in 1980. We believe that environmental responsibility is critically important today and tomorrow. Instead of hyperbole and sensationalism, we recruit America's best policy graduates to help present real data to policy makers about responsible environmental planning.

The internship is a stepping-stone to full-time employment at World Helper Institute. (Seven of our thirteen full-time policy analysts began their work as interns.) As a policy intern, you'll be given full access to our comprehensive library and resources on environmental policy. You will support the policy analysts in their research, including fact-checking reports, creating presentations for policy makers, and writing materials for our Web site. In addition, all interns specialize in one area: outreach, policy analysis, or project development.

Communicates what the position is and why it's meaningful.

Outreach:

The outreach specialization involves, for example, redesigning our Web site, creating brochures, and designing presentations for policy makers. Your goal will be to share our research findings with the outside world.

Policy analysis:

The policy analysis specialization involves working in-depth with our policy analysts to understand their emerging research. You may do fieldwork, interview experts in policy, or even write policy proposals that will be seen by decision makers.

Project development:

Interns who specialize in project development help create internal resources that make the institute more effective at our mission. For example, two past projects involved creating an intranet of shared materials for our policy analysts and organizing research materials to be accessible to the public.

This is the same position as the earlier job description, but this description makes the position much more attractive. Candidates are looking for areas to specialize in—not only because they will gain in-depth skills, but because they can tell others about exactly what they'll be doing.

REQUIREMENTS:

You'll need basic computer skills, including PowerPoint and Excel. But, more important, you'll need to be as passionate about environmental policy and demonstrate that to us. It may be in the form of classes taken or an organization you've founded, but we want to know what you've done to advance your passion—and why it's important to you.

INTERNSHIP DETAILS:

Depending on financial need, small stipends are available. The internship takes place in downtown Washington, D.C., from June 30 to September 1. To apply, please send your résumé and a cover letter to Beth Thomas, executive director of the World Helper Institute, at beth@worldhelperinstitute.com. She can also be reached at (202) 555-5555. Application deadline is March 1.

WHY APPLY?

The World Helper Institute summer policy internship is an excellent way to experience and contribute to a policy institute. You'll learn from some of the best analysts in the field (most of whom began as summer policy interns), and you'll specialize in one area (outreach, policy analysis, or project development) that will develop your skills for the future. Previous policy analysts have advanced within the institute. Some have gone on to law school, while others have remained in public service in the general area of policy analysis.

Last year, three of our major initiatives on global warming and environmental responsibility were passed into law.

The World Helper Institute was formed because we want to make a difference in the world—our mission of environmental responsibility is important to every single one of us at the institute. If you'd like to make a change—and see the results—we welcome you to apply.

This job description properly does not focus on compensation and benefits because there are few. Instead, it focuses on the mission and importance of the work being done.

Job Ads

Has anyone ever called you crazy?

What if you moved to another country,

to live with people you didn't know?

What if you went to improve their lives,

and in the process, improved yours.

Would that be crazy?

Peace Corps.
Life is calling.
How far will you go?

800.424.8580 | peacecorps.gov

A carefully thought-out ad by the Peace Corps uses evocative questions to appeal to the exact audience who would consider joining: young people who crave an unusual experience and want to have an impact on the world. Notice the ad's copy reassures the reader that, yes, it's okay to be different: "Has anyone ever called you crazy?"

The short, quick copy is perfect for young people who are used to reading blogs and Facebook and instant-messaging simultaneously. Note that the sentences don't have to be complete; they just have to resonate with young people. Finally, the images show the chance to be part of an exotic experience. And the ad offers a simple way to follow up: by phone or Web.

YOU COULD DO ANYTHING.
But where will you make the most impact in the world of retail?

How do you make the most impact in your career? We believe it is by joining a diverse team and sharing your expertise. At Montegi, we're leading the way forward to innovative fashion. But we need a culture of diverse thinkers who challenge the status quo. If you're looking to make a difference in the retail world in business development, finance, marketing, or operations, please join us at our information session on December 5.

Information session: Boscumb Hall, December 5, 5:00 P.M.–6:00 P.M. Business casual. Refreshments served.

These generic ads have become a favorite of consulting firms and investment banks; unfortunately, other organizations have started to pick up the trend. These ads usually have a broad, general statement about students ("You could do anything," "You decide," "You want to make a difference") and more platitudes about students and the interesting challenges they can face. If you already have a strong recruiting brand like Goldman Sachs, almost any ad can help reinforce your name, just like endless Coca-Cola ads on television. But if you are lesser known, you'll need to be more creative and specific to capture attention. For example, D.E. Shaw is a secretive financial firm that most people have never heard of. But Shaw recruits top candidates from top schools with the help of ad copy like this:

> It isn't always clear to people at first that they're right for the D.E. Shaw group. Like the poet we hired to head an automated block trading unit. Or the woman who designs solar-powered race cars; we hired her to help launch a new venture in computational

chemistry. They didn't think of themselves as "financial types," and neither did we. We thought of them as people with extraordinary talent.*

If we ran a company and our research told us that candidates were not applying because they didn't consider themselves "financial types," that is exactly the copy we'd use. It compels everyone to imagine how they could be great for D.E. Shaw, and it does so in a simple, concise way.

Simplicity is a fine line. The Montegi retail ad on page 259 is overly simple with few supporting details. Again, if you're a big name, this can work. But for most, it's not enough. On the other hand, if you write every detail about your available jobs, that's an essay or a full job posting, not an ad. Your ad should address the fears and hopes of your recruits so they take the next step—no more and no less. The single purpose of a job ad is to have your recruits get in touch with you.

And remember to test your ads. This can be as simple as going to the career center and asking to be introduced to ten students. Share multiple versions of the ads to those students and get their feedback. Don't forget to ask your new employees who are just out of college to weigh in as well. You can quickly eliminate the bad versions and focus on optimizing the best ones. When you find the winning ad and measure where your applications came from, you'll be able to improve subsequent ads and your overall recruiting campaign.

---

* http://www-tech.mit.edu/V125/PDF/N37.pdf

ACKNOWLEDGMENTS

FROM THE AUTHORS

To Lisa DiMona, Karen Watts, and Robin Dellabough at Lark Productions: If you ever want to write a book, call them first. We can't imagine that there's anyone better at what they do.

To the folks at Portfolio: Publisher Adrian Zackheim for taking a chance on us, Adrienne Schultz and Cathy Dexter for editing, Will Weisser and Courtney Nobile for getting the word out.

To the MIT UPOP team, especially Devon Biondi, Lora Chamberlain, Janna O'Neill, Liz Arnold, and Ronda Devine.

To the MIT students who helped so much with research and logistics: Erin Wei, Warren Bates, Philip Garcia, and Christian Rodriguez.

A special thanks to Mike Vasquez, who always did more than we asked.

And to Christopher Sawyer-Laucanno for believing in us from the beginning.

To Greg Harman, Eric Dauler, Brooke Roberts, Hadi Solh, Maggie Devine-Sullivan, Ann Cromer, and Mariangela Powley for their time and thoughts on our early proposals.

And to the thousands of students, employers, and university staff who so kindly shared their recruiting stories and experience. You taught us so much. Thanks to Elizabeth Reed and Christopher Pratt for so many introductions.

INDIVIDUAL THANKS

CHRIS—To my parents, William and Carmen Resto. Love you. To all my teachers for giving me knowledge and inspiring me to continue seeking more on my own, especially Ms. Charla-Ann Henderson, Ms. Margaret Rice, Ms. Renee Thomas, Ms. Dale McCall, Ms. Deborah Polson, Ms. Nona Kramer, Ms. Havela Drucker, Ms. Carmen Campbell, Ms. Carol McLean, and Ms. Barcia-Cook. My former colleagues and friends from Gemini Consulting and Capgemini. My good and talented neighbors in the MIT Careers Office. A thousand thanks to Jaishree and Desh Deshpande for the generosity that launched MIT UPOP, and to Tom Magnanti, Dick Yue, and Karl Reid for giving me the opportunity to make so much impact so early in my career.

IAN—To my parents, Peggy and Jesse Ybarra, for teaching me to read and then showing me so many books and movies that made me want to write my own, respectively. To Christopher Sawyer-Laucanno for making writing fun again. To B. D. Colen for kicking me out of class. To my favorite writers, Tahl Raz and Seth Godin, for challenging me to write more. And to Chris Resto, Thea Singer, Akshay Patil, Mike Hofman, Loren Feldman, and Keith Ferrazzi for giving me my first opportunities to write things that mattered.

RAMIT—To my parents, Prabhjot and Neelam Sethi. I'll never forget hearing you say, "Why don't you write that up?" To my English teacher Mrs. Shelton, who taught me that writing is about more than using the right words. To B.J. Fogg, George Northup, Meetpaul Singh, and Seth Godin, who gave me more latitude than I deserved and taught me how to get things done. And to my friends: I always love hearing about your recruiting adventures.

INDEX

academic department headquarters, 104

Accenture, 156

administrators, department, 104

ads, job, *see* job postings

Advanced Electron Beams, 69

advertising, 92, 213, 224
  for career fairs, 116
  mistakes made in, 125–28
  tracking effectiveness of, 213–14

Agamatrix, 130

alumni, 124
  lack of, 231

alumni associations, 96

Amazon.com, 182

AMS Consulting, 65–66

Apple, 46, 58, 69, 182

Applied Materials, 28, 140

Apprentice, The, 40, 96

Arnold, Liz, 187

athletic department, 108

A.T. Kearney, 156

awards, 52–53

Axelrod, Beth, 201, 218

backstage access, 49, 60

bad press about company, 239

Bain & Company, 17, 60–61, 78, 106, 109, 111, 134, 156
  first-round interviews for, 141
  new hires at, 169

Black Ops Entertainment, 171

Blackstone, 69–70

blogs, 77, 163, 258

Boeing, 7, 57

Boeing Satellite Systems, 37–38

books, sending to recruits, 48

Bose, 58, 60

Boston Consulting Group (BCG), 56, 71–72, 106

Bridgewater Associates, 30

budget cycle, 223

bulletin boards, 126
business schools, 27, 38

capstone courses, 165
career advancement, 25–26, 28,
    29–32, 79, 179, 204–5, 206,
    232–33, 235–36
  awarding new titles and/or
    promotions, 29
  coaching and support for, 31–32,
    133, 145
  increased or new responsibilities,
    29–30
  increasing compensation, 30–31
  recognition for achievements, 31
  stories of, in your company, 20,
    38–39, 48, 123, 133, 204, 235
career counselors, 105, 155
career fairs, 99, 114–21
  seminars on making the most of,
    107, 112
career offices, 100
careers, 13–32
  advancement in, *see* career
    advancement
  aspirations in, 14–16
  coaching and advice for, 31, 133
  commitment and, 16–22, 28, 39
  company mentor and, 177
  exposure to different paths in,
    21–25, 206
  managing of, 175–76
  paths in, 18, 79, 133, 145, 171,
    177, 235
  of predecessors in company, 20,
    38–39, 48, 123, 124, 133, 235
care packages, 48, 69, 158

Cirnigliaro, David, 4
classrooms and laboratories, 103–4
Clemente, Matt, 107
clubs, 107
Coca-Cola Scholars Foundation,
    93–94
college alumni associations, 96
colleges:
  alumni from, 124, 231
  choosing, 87–92
  elite, 89, 231
  extending reach beyond target
    schools, 92–96
  familiarity with, 97–98, 231
  peer, 231
Columbia University, 138
communicating with new hires,
    172–76
company culture and community,
    57–58, 73, 91–92, 181–83,
    240
company mentors, 176, 177, 178
compensation, increases in, 30–31
competence, of recruiters, 220
competitions, 104–6
competitiveness and exclusivity,
    40–44, 69–70, 140, 143, 237
CompuCom, 75
confidence, in recruiters, 219–20
Connery, Sean, 60
consulting firms, 23, 46, 49, 59–60,
    107, 111, 156, 171, 182, 202,
    203, 206
contact, 84
control, recruiters and, 220
conversion rates, 212, 215
co-op programs, 100–101

courtesy and class, 85, 210–11
customers, interaction with, 51

day-in-the-life workshops, 110,
    112
Deloitte Career Connections
    (DCC), 176
Deloitte Consulting, 139, 176
Denver University, 92
Deodato, Rick, 4
D.E. Shaw, 62, 259–60
desperation, 70, 140, 237–38
dinners and lunches, 48, 146, 182
diversity recruiting, 209–11
Dynegy, 100

EchoStar, 208
EG&G, 218
elevator pitch, 131
e-mail, 61–62, 104, 116, 126, 162,
    191
    autoresponders and, 191
    career fairs and, 120–21
    information sessions and, 122
    newsletters, 53
Emory University, 34
employees:
    bragging by, 203
    coworker relationships, 205
    exposure to, 144
    new, *see* new hires
    turning into evangelists and
        scouts, 188–92
    young, 55–56, 73
engineering schools, 27
enthusiasm, 78, 90
Ernst & Young, 35

events, 107, 109–12, 182, 183, 191
    advertising of, 125–28
    interviews and, 141
    scheduling of, 98
executives:
    books by, 48
    in recruiting efforts, 45–46, 69,
        217–18
externships, 101–2
extracurricular/learning time,
    24–25
Exxon, 55–56, 147–48

Facebook, 67, 258
Fast Company, 18
feedback:
    from interns, 185–88, 229–30
    on job postings, 260
feedback loop, 185–96
    turning employees and prospects
        into evangelists and scouts,
        188–92
Ferrazzi, Keith, 187
final exams, 48, 69, 158
Foley, Michelle, 109
food, free, 34, 58, 69, 109, 182

Gates, Bill, 4
GE Aircraft Engines (GEAE), 27
Gemini Consulting (Capgemini), 2,
    3, 4, 59, 62, 106, 112, 123, 146,
    164
General Atomics, 4
General Electric, 23
    leadership programs at, 42
General Electric Aviation, 101, 189
General Motors, 7, 99, 139

Georgia Tech, 47
glamour, 34, 44–45, 47–49, 50, 54, 64, 133, 140
goals, recruiting, 211–16
Goldman Sachs, 1, 2, 3, 5–8, 14, 30, 55, 57, 182
  business schools and, 27
  feedback and, 77
  recruit attributes and, 208
  salaries at, 35, 36
Google, 43, 87, 129, 201, 240
  Founders' Awards at, 30
  GPAs and, 215
  independent projects at, 24
  lectures at, 25
  perks and company culture at, 57–58, 134, 182
Google Alerts, 77
Google Blogsearch, 77
Gordon and Betty Moore Foundation, 169
gossip, 65–80, 118, 140, 143, 163, 175
  horror stories, 74–76
graduate school, 20, 26–27, 28, 37–38, 60, 133, 232–33
Guidant, 16
Gupta, Kunal, 95

Handfield-Jones, Helen, 201, 218
Harvard Business School, 27
Harvard University, 40, 106
Heyroth, Angela, 91–92, 208
Hispanic Scholarship Fund, 94
Hockfield, Susan, 15
horror stories, 74–76
hosts, 145, 148

housing, 164, 183–84, 231
HR, 224
  hiring managers and, 179–80, 224
  recruiting team and, 222–25

IBM, 63, 96
  Extreme Blue progam at, 41
Impact, 95–96
IncTank, 51
information sessions, 109, 112, 121–25, 129
Infosys, 59
Infusion Angels, 96
international assignments, 59–60
interns, 182, 205, 241–42
  coordinating projects for, 166–67
  enthusiasm of, 78–79
  feedback from, 185–88, 229–30
  as indispensable, 50–51
  past, hiring only, 215
  as recruiters, 189
  return of, 39, 43, 49, 183, 192–93, 204, 229–30
internships, 100–101
  advertising of, 127
  career fairs and, 119
  competitive, 41, 44
  of competitor, 236–38
  deadlines for accepting or declining, 154, 155
  externships and job shadow programs, 101–2
  problems with, 229–30
interviews, 92, 136–48, 150
  final-round on-site, 144–48
  first-round on-campus, 140–44
  mock, 111

offers and, *see* offers
  timing of, 137–40
Intuit, 23
  Rotational Development
    Program at, 57
investment banks, 49, 59, 68,
    126–27, 147, 156, 182, 201–2,
    237
"I want YOU" sentiment, 61–64

Jarvis, Rebecca, 40
Jet Propulsion Laboratories, 194
job offers, *see* offers
job postings, 92, 99, 128–34,
    243–60
  advertising of, 125–28
  critiques of, 243–57
  feedback on, 260
  format for, 128, 130–34
  generic, 259, 260
  Peace Corps, 243, 258
  writing style in, 134
job shadow programs, 101–2
job titles:
  in job postings, 127, 130–31
  new, awarding, 29
Johnson & Johnson, 25, 58

Kiwanis Club, 94
Kraft, Bob, 218
Kronos, 190–91

leadership development, 21, 23,
    27–28, 31, 57
  accelerated programs for, 42, 44
lectures and seminars, 25
Lehman Brothers, 29, 153

life outside of work, 145, 147–48,
    183–84, 205, 230–31
Lions Clubs, 94
L.L. Bean, 103
locale, 53–55, 56–57, 88, 91, 230–31
Ludwig, Eugene, 46
luxury items, offering to recruits,
    49

McKinsey & Company, 1, 2, 3, 5–8,
    12, 14, 15, 17, 43, 45, 55, 87,
    97, 106, 127, 137, 160, 170,
    182, 200, 201, 217, 219
  alumni program at, 31
  backstage access at, 60
  business analyst program at, 27
  business schools and, 27, 38
  exposure to numerous projects at,
    22, 23
  information sessions of, 125
  personal contact and, 62
  salaries at, 35, 36
  "sell" weekends at, 157
  skills and, 207
Macquarie, 59
management consulting firms, 111,
    156, 171, 202, 203, 206
management skills, 24, 30
managers:
  HR and, 179–80, 224
  as mentors, 176–77, 230
  new hires and, 162, 163
Medtronic, 16, 148
Meehan, Emily, 55
mentors, 176–79, 230
Merrill Lynch, 150
messengers, 77–78

metrics, 215–16
Michaels, Ed, 201, 218
Microsoft, 1–8, 11, 12, 14, 18, 36,
    45, 53, 75, 87, 97, 137, 160,
    182, 193, 195, 200, 201, 214,
    217, 219, 220
  alumni of, in leadership positions,
    27–28
  attention to detail at, 72
  competitive recruiting and, 42, 43
  contact with recruits, 84
  exposure to numerous projects at,
    22
  feedback and, 77
  program manager position at, 24
  skills and talent and, 208–9
  quality of work at, 49
  work environment at, 182
Mikva Challenge, 70–71
Minneapolis, Minn., 56–57
minorities, 209–11
mistakes, 80
MIT (Massachusetts Institute of
    Technology), 1–2, 4, 11–12, 15,
    16, 20, 22, 43, 65, 69, 107–8,
    123, 199–200, 207
  interns from, 186–87
  job e-mail list at, 104
MIT UPOP (Undergraduate
    Practice Opportunities
    Program), 2, 8, 101, 138, 187,
    213
Model United Nations, 95
money, 35–37, 68, 136
  bonuses, 36
  pay raises, 30–31
  salary negotiations, 156

Morgan Stanley, 25, 29, 153
  competitive recruiting and,
    43

Nadal, Daphne, 105
National Association of Colleges
    and Employers (NACE), 4,
    214
National Scholarship Providers
    Association, 94
National Society of Black
    Engineers, 95
national student organizations,
    95–96
networks, 180
new hires:
  communicating with, 172–76
  losing, after two years, 232–33
  management of, 160–84
  mentors for, 176–79, 230
  networking and, 180
  recognition for, 52–53
  as recruiters, 46–47, 222
  talent development and, 179–80
  see also career advancement;
    careers; work
Northeastern University, 100–101

offers, 148–59, 237–38
  accepted, celebrating, 158–59
  bonuses for accepting by a certain
    date, 155, 193, 238
  deadlines for accepting or
    declining, 154–56, 238–39
  earning of, 140
  going over details of, 151–52
  postoffer management, 161–64

rejections of, 195–96
salary negotiations in, 156
"sell" weekends and, 156–58
timing of, 238
what students think about, 152–56
O'Neill, Janna, 100
open houses, 110, 112–13
Oracle PeopleSoft, 190–91

parties and social events, 60–61, 69
patents, 52
Peace Corps, 26, 37, 243, 258
performance reviews, 180–81
PerkinElmer, 218
perks, 57–61, 68–69, 134
personal contact, 61–62, 231
PGA Tour, 69
phone calls, 61–62, 79, 120, 141,
    162
  offers and, 150–51, 158
Pinkett, Randal, 40
Pinson, Jennifer, 42
Pitney Bowes, 75
posters, 126
Power Systems Manufacturing,
    218
Princeton University, 34, 47
Procter & Gamble, 54, 240
products and services, 51–52
  credit for contributions to, 171
  offering to recruits, 58–59
progress reports, 174–75
Promontory Financial Group, 46
promotions, 29, 78
publications, new hires and, 52
publicizing accomplishments of new
    hires, 53

Rasmus, Dan, 18
Raytheon, 125
receptions, 146
recognition for achievements, 31,
    52–53
recruiters, 217–25
  employees and prospects as,
    188–92
  executives as, 45–46, 69,
    217–18
  HR and, 222–25
  qualities needed in, 218–20
  recent hires as, 46–47, 222
  recruiting more, 221–22
  top guns as, 45–47, 69
  training of, 225
recruiting:
  advice for problems with, 229–42
  contact in, 84
  courtesy and class in, 85
  defining your target recruit in,
    207–9
  diversity, 209–11
  for noncore functional groups,
    234–36
  selling people first, company
    second in, 84–85
  setting goals for, 211–16
  top spots for, 99–109
rejections, 193–94
reputation, and bad news about
    company, 239
Research in Motion, 96
residential life, 108–9
responsibilities, 71
  diverse set of, 24
  increased or new, 29–30

résumés:
  critiques of, 101, 110
  technology for managing, 190, 191
  timing of interviews and, 137–38
Ron Brown Scholars Program, 94
Ross, Patti, 93–94
Rotary Clubs, 94
rotation programs, 21, 22–23, 28,
    140, 179

salaries, 35–37, 68, 136
  negotiating, 156
  pay raises, 30–31
scheduling and timing:
  of events, 98
  in interview process, 137–40
  of offers, 238
Schlumberger, 103, 142, 178
scholarship programs, 93–95
scientific research companies, 170
Scott, Mary, 214
Scott Resource Group, 214
self-assessment, 202–7, 233–34
self-confidence, in recruiters,
    219–20
"sell" weekends, 156–58
seminars and lectures, 25
Shafi Inc., 50–51
SilkRoad technology, 190–91
skills, 89–90, 207, 208–9
  new, learning, 169–70, 175, 206
small companies, 240–42
Society for Human Resource
    Management (SHRM), 214
Society of Hispanic Professional
    Engineers, 95
Sorenson-Wagner, Mark, 155

speakers, at career fairs, 123
speaking engagements, for new
    hires, 52
special project assignments, 23–24
special treatment, 73–74
start-up companies, 240–42
State Department, U.S., 95
student groups, 95–96, 107–8, 191
student leaders, 47
student living groups, 108–9
Summe, Greg, 218
superconnectors, 98–99, 102, 110,
    113, 116, 122, 126, 238

talent, 207, 208–9
  development of, 179–80
  refilling the pipeline, 192–96
TD Banknorth, 103
Teach For America, 20, 95, 190
technology, as recruiting aid, 190–91
Technorati, 77
TELUS Communications, 96
Thomson West, 31, 57, 73–74, 146
timing and scheduling:
  of events, 98
  in interview process, 137–40
  of offers, 238
titles:
  in job postings, 127, 130–31
  new, awarding, 29
Toyota, 95
transportation, 164, 183
travel, 59, 68–69, 133
  international assignments,
    59–60
Trump, Donald, 40
tuition reimbursement, 37–38, 133

UBS, 112, 168
UCLA, 34, 107
University of California at Irvine,
    105, 109
University of Houston, 100
University of Minnesota, 106, 155
University of Pennsylvania, 15
University of Southern Maine,
    103
U.S. Department of Education, 192

values, 89, 203
Vault.com, 163
Virginia Tech, 4

Walker, Ernest, 99
Wall Street, 26, 35, 68, 202
Wall Street Journal, 55
War for Talent, The (Michaels,
    Handfield-Jones, and Axelrod),
    201, 218
Web sites, 53, 77, 163
Westat, 192
Wetfeet.com, 163
Wharton School, 102
Wilson, Randy, 211
work, 49–50, 70–71, 144–45,
    164–72
  changing projects, 206
  communication and, 172–76

coordinating projects, 166–67
credit for, 171
expectations about, 173–74, 175
extracurricular/learning time and,
    24–25
importance and quality of, 49,
    160, 165–66, 167–68, 205, 230,
    235
learning new skills in, 169–70,
    175
mentors and, 176–79
open-ended projects, 169
owning projects, 167
performance reviews and, 180–81
preparation for, 161–64
progress reports and, 174–75
project wrap-ups, 175
responsibilities in, 24, 29–30
showing to candidates, 147
special project assignments,
    23–24
starting a project, 172–74
variety in, 170–71
see also careers
work environment, 25, 57–58, 73,
    205

Xerox, 171–72

Yahoo!, 25

ABOUT THE AUTHORS

CHRIS RESTO is the founding director of MIT's largest internship program, the School of Engineering's Undergraduate Practice Opportunities Program (UPOP), to which he will donate his portion of the royalties from *Recruit or Die*. He has advised hundreds of companies and thousands of college students on recruiting. Resto earned his bachelor's degree in civil engineering from MIT and returned to start UPOP after working for the Paris-based strategy firm Gemini Consulting (now Capgemini). In Gemini's strategic research group, Resto recruited and managed new college graduates from top universities. He lives in Boston.

IAN YBARRA graduated from MIT in 2004 with a bachelor's degree in materials science and engineering. As an undergraduate, he assisted Resto with starting UPOP at MIT and held internships with Gemini Consulting, General Electric Aviation, and IncTank Ventures. After college, he helped business relationships expert Keith Ferrazzi with editing and marketing his best-selling book, *Never Eat Alone*. He has written for *Inc.* magazine, *Forbes.com*, *FastCom-*

pany.com, *Monster.com*, and the auspicious MIT *Tech*. He continues to write about doing what you love at IanYbarra.com. He lives in Smallville, Kansas.

RAMIT SETHI graduated from Stanford University in 2005 with bachelor's and master's degrees in technology, psychology, and sociology. During college, he interviewed dozens of students about career decisions and advised several employers on how to attract the best and the brightest. After interning with business author Seth Godin, Sun Microsystems, and AuctionDrop, he received full-time job offers from Google, Intuit, and Andor Capital. He is now cofounder and vice president of marketing for PBwiki, an online start-up in Silicon Valley. He teaches personal finance to young people on his blog IWillTeachYouToBeRich.com, which has been featured in the *Wall Street Journal* and the *New York Times*, and in seminars across the country. He lives in San Francisco.